'If it be now, 'tis not to come;
if it be not to come, it will be now.'

Hamlet, Act 5, Scene 2

The D-Word:
Talking about Dying

A Guide for Relatives,
Friends and Carers

SUE BRAYNE

continuum

Published by the Continuum International Publishing Group
The Tower Building, 11 York Road, London SE1 7NX
80 Maiden Lane, Suite 704, New York NY 10038

www.continuumbooks.com

Copyright © Sue Brayne, 2010

First published 2010

British Library Cataloguing-in-Publication Data
A catalogue record for this book is available from the British Library.

ISBN 978-1-4411-8679-9

Designed and typeset by Kenneth Burnley, Wirral, Cheshire
Printed and bound by the MPG Books Group

Contents

Acknowledgements

First and foremost, heartfelt love and appreciation go to Dr Peter Fenwick and Elizabeth Fenwick, without whom this book could not have come into being. I would also like to thank all those at Continuum Books, especially Andrew Walby, a pleasure to work with, and Robin Baird-Smith, for his willingness to engage with the D-Word. Profound thanks also to Roberta Smith for her illustrations, and Kenneth Burnley for his design.

I am most grateful to Professor Tony Walter for his generous contribution. To Dr Adrian Clarke for his professional eye. To Professor Sheila Payne for her support. To Joan Sewell from the Metropolitan Police for her expertise on breaking bad news. To Clare Gittings for her awesome historical knowledge. And to Professor Carol Brayne for her generosity of spirit.

Sincere thanks also to Sally Eden, Pauline Williams, Sarah Cunliffe, Dr Morag Farquhar and to Dr Jane Fleming for invaluable suggestions on the manuscript. To Janie and Nancy who saved the day, and to Lorraine Mitchell and Caro Gozen for such warmth and encouragement.

Special gratitude and recognition go to all of you who told me your stories. This book could not have happened without you. And exceptional thanks to my husband, Mark, who is always there. No matter what.

A note on the cover

The ash tree symbolizes how we are innately connected not just to each other, but also to all the systems and patterns of the natural world.

Holding this awareness helps us to learn about ourselves as we journey through life.

Talking about the D-Word

Alys, aged 54

Every few days I write to people I know and tell them what it's been like for me. I feel I need to educate them about the D-Word and about cancer. How else are they going to learn? You don't read about this unless you are terminally ill yourself, or you are an academic or a palliative care specialist.

I have been diagnosed with stage three colon cancer. I don't think of myself as being sick: I think of myself as having a diagnosis. I don't want to be defined by the cancer, or by chemotherapy. But whether you like it or not, having it does change your relationships.

I was very careful about how I told my children, but I have been much more relaxed with friends. Some have been fantastic. Others are literally shattered by the news, or can't handle it at all. I can understand that, but it's been quite hard when I really wanted a particular friend to be there for me. She simply can't do it.

Quite a few people respond by saying things like 'You'll be fine – I know you will.' On the one hand, it helps me to see a future in which I will be fine. On the other, of course, they don't know I will be fine – especially with such a diagnosis.

What has been the most helpful is having friends and family who are willing to spend time with me, and being okay with what's happening to me.

I don't see what has happened as a punishment or a judgement. I am frightened of pain, but I am not afraid of dying. I would like to have a spiritually conscious death – to know I am dying, to be able to say all my goodbyes, and to embrace the dying moment.

I haven't felt sad either. I have so much love around me from family and friends. So maybe I haven't had time, or I just don't feel it. My cancer has instilled a deep sense of gratitude in me. I am so grateful to have seen my children grow up. I am also deeply grateful for what I have each day. It makes me live in the moment.

At the same time, I have had to learn to compromise. Initially I did not want to have chemotherapy – I have seen what it can do to others suffering from cancer. But my children and my husband thought otherwise. I didn't want them to feel angry with me for not trying to save my life.

Therefore, I have had to change my perception of chemotherapy from a toxic poison to a healer. So when I go for treatments I talk to my cancer, and invite in my healer and surrender to what I call a divine devouring fire. It makes it much easier.

Welcome to the D-Word

The word 'Dying' – the D-Word – carries with it a weighty load. Fear, despair and beauty. Loneliness, dread and hope. Love, remorse and helplessness. Mess, smell, noise and ugliness. Separation, reunion, union. Finality, pain, loss. Controversy, release, relief, grief. Perhaps it is this complex mix which makes it hard for many of us to talk openly and honestly about the dying experience.

In earlier times, death and dying took place within a much clearer social, political and religious context. People knew how to recognize the approach of death, how to talk about it and how to support those who were dying. Today, dying is a very different experience. Most of us will die in hospital, and while the medicalization of death provides structure at a time of uncertainty and fear, it does little to help us face the emotional challenge of dealing with the actual dying experience, whether our own or someone else's.

By the very nature of the subject, this book will raise many more questions than it can possibly hope to answer. But this is not an academic or scientific study. Nor does it focus on bereavement, funerals, questions about the afterlife, the moral debate of euthanasia and assisted suicide, or the care of those suffering from dementia. Those subjects are catered for elsewhere.

The D-Word is based on the lived, felt, human experience of what it's like to die. For that reason, I hope that this book will serve as a companion and guide to help anyone who wants to learn more about the language of dying, or needs support as they face the end of life of someone close, or perhaps would like to prepare for the inevitability of their own death.

Personal stories

Talking about the end of life involves issues that are broad and complicated. However, drawing on my own experiences of sitting with the dying, I have chosen to explore the end of life through the personal narratives of relatives, friends and carers who have coped with the dying process of a spouse, a parent, a friend or a child – how they confronted their fear of talking about it, and how they found support during what can be a very difficult and distressing time.

I have also spoken with academics, doctors and nurses about the professional experience of what it is like to work with the dying and their relatives. And I have interviewed faith leaders to explore their personal perceptions of our spiritual relationship with the D-Word.

Some interviewees have given permission to be identified. Others, with a view to the sensitivity of their stories and a concern not to upset relatives, have asked for their name to be changed. To respect this, and for consistency, names have either been changed or I have used first names only.

When sitting with the dying, all the interviewees said they had learned something important not just about the D-Word but also about themselves. Sometimes the experience changed their lives. Sometimes there was just a sharpening of awareness about their own mortality. But I was particularly struck by their eagerness to talk about the D-Word. Far from being taboo, it helped me to understand that, given the chance, most people are in fact aching to tell their story. Colin Murray-Parker, British psychiatrist and author of numerous books on grief, remarked, 'It's not that our society denies death, it's just we are ignorant of it.'

As a result, this book contains a collection of extraordinary, yet at the same time also rather ordinary, accounts about the dying experience. Many interviewees shared similar stories, but felt alone or isolated because they had never spoken about it before. Once they realized this, a typical response was, 'It makes me feel a lot better to know I am not the only one to think or feel like that.'

Speaking as the narrator of these stories, the writing of *The D-Word* turned into a profound journey of exploration about how important it is to communicate or, at the very least, acknowledge end-of-life issues. Far from being gloomy or depressing, I hope this journey will help you, the reader – whether relative, friend or carer – to find better ways of talking about all aspects of the dying experience.

To complement this book, the D-Word website (www.d-word.co.uk) has been set up to provide further information, including personal stories, information on workshops, medical information and links to organizations that deal with death and dying.

Structure

The book is divided into eight separate chapters, each of which can be read on its own, or in sequence as part of the whole book.

Chapter 1 looks at the effect that the denial of the D-Word has on us as individuals and our spiritual well-being. It also explores the wider implications of how death-denying behaviour affects the way we treat the natural world.

Chapter 2 is a historical view of how the development of Western culture has led to the sanitization and medicalization of the D-Word. The chapter also questions how we as a society learn about death and dying, and considers how the media influence our thinking about end-of-life issues.

Chapter 3 investigates the D-Word from a medical perspective. Three doctors and three nurses provide insights about their work with the dying, from providing medical support and making crucial end-of-life decisions, to the importance of good communication skills, and caring for the elderly.

Chapter 4 considers where faith and spirituality can help us face the death of a close relative or friend, and how it can also comfort the dying. Representatives from five different faiths talk about their perception of the D-Word, and how they have drawn on their beliefs to help them personally and professionally.

Chapter 5 looks at different ways of having *the* conversation. It also looks at what happens when resolution with a dying person is not possible, and examines the emotional toll on children when they are prevented from talking about the death of a close family member or friend.

Chapter 6 focuses on different aspects of the D-Word such as sudden or violent death, suicide and miscarriage. Six personal stories explore what helped and what did not help each individual, and how they experienced people responding to their grief.

Chapter 7 discovers different ways in which relatives, friends and carers have found help and support when coping with the D-Word. It also draws attention to the language of euphemisms and the fact that not everyone experiences grief. It concludes with practical guidance on how to break bad news.

Chapter 8 offers practical advice for relatives, friends and carers of the dying. It covers all aspects of the dying experience, from the need for good listening skills and how the body starts to shut down, to end-of-life experiences and what happens at the moment of death.

The Appendix looks at what can be done to tackle the D-Word, from bereavement support and education, to government policy and medical training.

The book concludes with a recommended reading list and some useful addresses.

A Personal Note

I cannot recall a time when I wasn't interested in death. Even as a child I wondered what became of us at the moment of death. I believe it was this that attracted me to train as a nurse during the early 1970s.

During my medical training, I do not remember a nursing tutor ever talking to us about any aspect of death and dying, or what it was like to sit with someone as they died. I cannot say that the subject was actively ignored, it just wasn't spoken about, even though my experience of nursing the dying led me to believe that there were many ways to die. For example, a few deaths had what I would describe as a spiritual quality to them. Some were much more prosaic, while others could be seen to be distressing, traumatic, or just terribly sad, especially when it involved a young person.

My first encounter with the dying experience came while I was on night duty. I was 19 at the time and on my own in a small ward. It was well after midnight and all was quiet. Yet something – I have no idea what this something was – made me put down the book I was reading in the nurse's station and go to a side room to check on an elderly lady.

I pushed open the door so see her lying on her back, quite peacefully. There was a rattling sound coming from her throat which at first I found puzzling. I then realized she was dying and was aware of feeling frightened. At that moment the room filled with the most beautiful, serene ambience. I stood at the door transfixed by it for several moments. I then felt an urgency to leave the room. I can remember hovering outside in the corridor not knowing what to do, before entering her room again. I went straight to her bedside and saw that she had died. The ambience intensified and, for me, the room seemed to fill with a kind of sparkling light. I was completely overwhelmed by the experience, and a hint of it stayed in the room long after a colleague and I had laid out her body. But at the time I did not speak about it to anyone.

In complete contrast, I remember rescuing an elderly patient wandering the corridor in a state of great agitation, the gap in his hospital gown exposing tired, yellowing flesh and an emaciated bottom. He died a few days later, thankfully with his family at his bedside to calm him. I also recall laying out a young man in his early thirties. He had a shock of red hair and lots of freckles all over his body, and I wondered who he was and what he might have become. While again on night duty, another elderly lady had a heart attack. The senior nurse and I valiantly tried to resuscitate her by giving her mouth-to-mouth, but she died anyway.

Still no one spoke about these deaths. We did our jobs and continued with our duties as if nothing had happened.

I left nursing shortly after I qualified because I wanted to break away from the discipline of hospital life and to explore different avenues of work – which I did until I reached my mid-thirties. At the time I was deeply unhappy, but did not have the emotional wherewithal to make the changes that I needed.

But change I did – and not in the way I expected. Death very nearly caught up with me one gorgeously warm August evening. I was sitting in a light aircraft, piloted by a friend, flying at 3,000 feet over southern England, when, out of the blue, the engine coughed a couple of times and stopped. I saw the colour drain from my friend's face and knew we were in serious trouble. He immediately began to send out mayday calls and to jettison fuel. I remember shutting my eyes tightly and started to say goodbye in my head to everyone I knew. It was very frightening, but also strangely freeing, because I knew there was nothing I could do about what was going to happen. As we lost height, I recall opening my eyes to see the top of a bank of trees coming towards us, and saying to my friend, 'We're going to make it.'

'No we are not,' he said. A second later we hit the trees. I remember being thrown around in my seat as the plane spun round and fell to the ground, then shards of glass from the windscreen showered onto my lap. The instant I realized I was still alive, my friend shouted at me to get out of the plane as it was going to blow up. Somehow I scrambled out of the wreckage and found myself sitting on the grass, unscathed but in profound shock. It felt as if my skin had been metaphorically torn off, leaving me raw and very vulnerable. During the weeks that followed I experienced a suicidal depression. I could barely get out of bed, and was forced to face the truth that I had wasted years trying to be someone I was not, and that my life had neither meaning or purpose.

It was shortly after this that I had a profound mystical experience which changed my life. I was lying on the sofa when a sentence dropped into my head. 'You will become a bereavement counsellor.' My depression instantly lifted and I sat up, realizing I had been given a second chance. Facing my own mortality had enabled me to reconnect with who I really was. It was now down to me if I wanted to take advantage of it or not.

This led me to embark on an intense 15-year healing journey, leading, via training with the Elisabeth Kübler-Ross Foundation as a life, death and transition facilitator, eventually to the completion of a Master's degree in the 'Rhetoric and Rituals of Death'. My MA introduced me to the work of Dr Peter Fenwick (neuroscientist and co-author, with his wife Elizabeth Fenwick, of the excellent *Art of Dying*). And, as they say, the rest is history.

Palliative care nurse Hilary Lovelace and I joined Peter to research 'end-of-life experiences' (see page 125). Our study has produced several academic papers and two end-of-life booklets, *End-of-Life Experiences: A Guide for Carers of the Dying* and *Nearing the End of Life: A Guide for Relatives and Friends of the Dying* (see page 167 to order copies).

During the time when I was writing the relatives' guide, my 87-year-old father died. He had often spoken about his death. In fact, we discussed it on the telephone the week before he was taken to hospital.

He said that he was worried about the prospect of going into a care home – and how much he wanted to go like his mother, who enjoyed robust health until she died a few days after suffering a stroke. I said, 'Well, Dad, you can't buy the way you die from Waitrose. You'll just have to ask for it.' A week later he had a massive stroke – indeed, just like his mother – and was rushed into hospital.

My father had always made my brother and me promise not to resuscitate him should his quality of life become severely impaired. A brain scan revealed a massive bleed, which had robbed him of his speech and sight and had paralyzed him down his right-hand side. He would never recover. So, we agreed with medical staff that life-prolonging treatment should stop.

Sitting with my father for the further six days it took for him to die transformed me from an impartial observer of end-of-life experiences and ex-nurse, into an exhausted, emotionally dazed daughter whose existence was turned upside down as I agonizingly waited for his life to end. A friend described sitting with her dying parent as a 'displacement of the soul'. I think that sums up exactly what it's like.

Professor Allan Kellehear, sociologist and author of *A Social History of Dying*, talks of how our fear of what we don't know – or are unprepared for – when accompanying someone during their dying process turns it into a 'death watch'. I certainly agree with this. But since I accepted that my father was dying, and because of my interest in end-of-life experiences, I was very alert to how my father might behave. So for me, his dying experience was anything but a death watch.

And he did not let me down. Although he was unable to move his right side, or communicate in any way, with his left hand he would often reach out in front of him as if taking hold of some kind of substance – or perhaps some kind of material – and then rub it between his thumb and fingers as if trying to work out what it was. My father was not on medication, so this was no drug-induced hallucination. He clearly knew what he was doing and it was not causing him distress.

As the days passed, he seemed to slip in and out of consciousness – but in what appeared to be his more lucid moments, he would often sit with his hand holding the side of his face as if in deep thought. Of course I can't know, but it felt to me that he was either being 'told something' or he was working something out deep inside.

My father still went through Cheyne-Stokes breathing, where breathing stops only to start again, and at times became agitated – but that's what the dying process is like – sometimes peaceful, sometimes distressed. Nevertheless my father seemed to be going through some kind of profound subjective experience which, to me, seemed to be preparing him for what was to come. I'm not sure I could call it a spiritual experience, because I wasn't aware of him connecting to a sense of the divine. But I certainly would call it existential in the way he appeared to be creating inner meaning for himself.

Witnessing my father's dying enriched my relationship with him – we had never been close – and was, for me, similar to what Dr Sherwin Nuland describes in his book, *How We Die*. 'Death', Nuland says, 'is not usually a time of wonderful experiences. But it is frequently a time of healing experiences.'

My father's openness about dying was a gift to me. But it is not always like this. All too often we don't know how to talk about end-of-life issues: how to behave or what to say. That is especially true of our Western culture, where talking about dying is still seen by many as a taboo.

This apparent taboo has inspired me to write *The D-Word*, partly to share my own personal experiences of the dying process, and partly because of my passion to confront the barriers that prevent us from talking honestly and openly about something that conclusively is going to happen to us all.

This book is dedicated to you, the reader.

'Doctor, do you think it could have been the sausage?'

French playwright, Paul Claudel, upon his deathbed

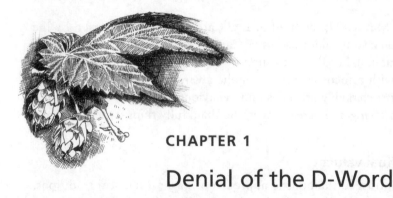

CHAPTER 1

Denial of the D-Word

We all live with a terminal diagnosis. It's called life. At the end of which we are going to die. This can happen to us at any age, and at any time. It can manifest as a terminal illness such as cancer. Or as a chronic disease, either acquired or inherited, or through infectious diseases, such as flu and cholera. Or our bodies just get old and wear out. People also die suddenly and violently, in accidents, wars, suicides, or in natural and man-made disasters. And it's important not to forget miscarriage or still-born babies who never fully make it into life at all.

Nonetheless, our fast-living modern culture does little to cater for the D-Word, nor does it encourage us to be aware of the fragility of life, or indeed to recognize the signs or language that indicate when death may be imminent.

However, before we consider what can help us to talk about dying, it's important to look at why many of us find this difficult, and why so many of us reach the end of our life without having really thought about death or truly prepared for it.

Out of the National Health Service's £100 billion annual budget, spending for dying patients is only a small fraction of this. A study conducted in 2008 by the organization Dignity in Dying revealed that, from 31 Primary Care Trusts across London, it was less than one-half of one per cent of their total funding.

To address this, in July 2008, the British Government announced that it was ready to invest £286 million in a new 'End of Life Care Strategy'. It is well needed. In 2007, the Healthcare Commission (the NHS watchdog), said that more than half of all complaints made against the NHS concerned end-of-life care.

In May 2009, the 'End of Life Care Strategy', supported by the National Council for Palliative Care, announced 'the formation of a new national coalition to support the implementation of this strategy, with a focus on raising public awareness and with an aim to support changing attitudes and behaviours in society in relation to death, dying and bereavement'. So thankfully things are changing.

Spiritual values

In contrast to the holistic approach of Eastern medical traditions, where the physical, mental and spiritual condition of the person is taken into account, Western medicine focuses primarily on the malfunctions of the body. Relatively little attention is given to the mental and spiritual well-being of the patient as part of their treatment.

Nevertheless, Britain's Royal College of Psychiatrists recognizes that spirituality is an essential part of the human condition, without which it is hard for us to find a sense of personal meaning, hope, purpose and belonging. This can be found through religious faith or spiritual practice such as prayer or meditation, or perhaps also through more secular activities like gardening, walking, running, even cooking. In fact, spirituality can be seen as whatever we do that helps to soothe and calm our mind so that we can heighten our understanding of life and the relationship between ourselves and the natural world of which we are a part.

Spirituality can enable us to make sense of our life and give us the inner resources to face difficult and challenging situations. There's much research to show how this need to make sense of life intensifies as we approach the end of life. If we are not provided with appropriate support and understanding, it can leave us in spiritual distress, feeling isolated, alone and frightened.

Spirituality for me is also linked with compassion, dignity and respect, especially when working with those approaching the end of life. I will never forget a doctor coming into my father's hospital side room a couple of days before he died, to assess his levels of consciousness. While shining a bright light into his eyes, the doctor shouted at him. When he didn't respond (he couldn't), she dug her thumb into his breast-bone, which made him moan with pain. I was horrified, but before I could stop her, she ran a sharp stick up the soles of both his feet, making him flinch and cry out again. The doctor concluded loudly in front of him that she didn't know how long he had to live, before sweeping out of the room. I realized that the doctor was carrying out standard medical tests for responsiveness to stimuli in an unconscious patient. But I found her lack of care and gentleness towards my father and towards me very upsetting.

An entitlement to life

The deficiency of spiritual values in today's Western society shows itself, it seems to me, as an inappropriate sense of *entitlement* to life. In fact, it could be argued that we no longer expect death to happen. Even the end of life for an elderly person can be regarded with shock. Not so long ago a friend called to tell me, in considerable distress, about the sudden and unexpected death of her friend's father. I was very sorry to hear what had happened, and asked how old he was. 'Eighty-eight,' came her reply. I am sure this man's family were deeply dismayed that he had died. But it did make me question how out of touch we have become as a society if the death of an 88-year-old is regarded as unexpected or, indeed, erroneous.

When we fail to engage with the reality of our mortality, we reject personal responsibility, for example: 'It's not my fault I've got lung cancer, even though I smoke 40 cigarettes a day.' Or we plead ignorance: 'I didn't know that eating only processed food was bad for my health.' Or we become helpless: 'I will hand myself over to the specialist. He/she will know what's best for me.'

We also decant blame: 'It's not my fault I've got cirrhosis of the liver – the Government shouldn't have increased the drinking hours.' Or we make others do the worrying: 'I don't want to know what's wrong with me. Someone else can worry about that.'

These examples may sound extreme, but we all have tendencies to behave like this when we refuse to accept or talk about our mortality.

The effect on the natural world

We can see how our death-denying behaviour can affect us on an individual level. But there are far-reaching implications when we project this denial onto the natural world. At the time of writing, it is increasingly evident that irresponsible and thoughtless human behaviour is causing serious change to the world's ecosystems. The implications of this could be catastrophic. Dr Rachel Stanworth, author of *Recognising Spiritual Needs in People Who Are Dying*, believes that unless we have an understanding of death, we are unable to build a healthy relationship with life. She told me,

> The apparent finality of death can be terrifying. When we deny death, however, life can lose its savour and meaning. This is not just about talking about death, it's about developing some sense of the furthest horizon against which we live. An horizon that may well extend beyond our own lifespan. It is through accepting death that we allow life to call us to a deeper understanding of ourselves; an awareness of our ultimate meaning, purpose and value. Without this we can end up cruelly and brutally exposed to our deepest fears.
>
> Sadly, Western culture gradually has less and less grounding in this type of awareness. Most people learn about death and dying through the distorted representations of television dramas. Many of us do not live in supportive communities and we end up going it alone. There is a real sense in which we have lost an authentic language of dying so that we no longer know how to surrender to powerlessness in any positive sense or with trust. A trust that everything will be all right even when we do not know what 'all right' will look like.

Jamie, a psychotherapist who lives in the south-east of England, agrees:

> In our culture, it seems to me that we talk about dying as if it doesn't exist. In fact, we deny it. Nowadays, people tend to regard themselves as omnipotent and all-powerful. Medical interventions are such that people live a lot longer, even in a disabled state. So dying is not regarded as a meaningful part of life.
>
> We are so possession-driven that people are trained to believe that the product is the answer – so they carry with them an ambivalence about life.
>
> Descartes' 'I think, therefore I am' has a lot to answer for. But I believe this mode of thinking is beginning to fall apart. Climate change, for instance, is forcing us to accept there are limitations to the market economy and to industrialization – those factors which have taken us out of our bodies, and away from ourselves. People are

being forced to face the realities of life – one of which is that we all die.

People are frightened of suffering – so what people mostly bring to me as a therapist is a fear of *how* they might die rather than the death itself. I have an elderly client who is learning to accept that her life is beginning to draw to an end. However, she is also aware that whatever happens next can be meaningful, and can become part of her life right now. That's the challenge for all of us.

Facing our dying ultimately makes us responsible. My certain knowledge that it's going to happen puts me at the centre of my life. Life doesn't happen to me – it's me who makes things happen in my life. I have the certainty of dying to remind me that I have only so long to get the hang of this. I find that exciting.

The environmentalist Mark Lynas, author of *Six Degrees* – a sobering account of what humanity is facing – also believes we have become increasingly disconnected from our planetary origins, with the result that people have lost respect for the living world. He told me:

When we buy ready-made meals, or all the other convenient ways we keep ourselves alive, we forget we are completely dependent on the living biosphere. There is a severing between our modern-self and our animal-self that evolved via the natural world.

The result of this severance means we have an inflated sense of self. We have lost that humility which comes with knowing that nature is in charge. We believe we are in charge, and this is why mortality appals us.

Modern medicine is so good at keeping us alive that there is almost a culture shock when someone dies. At the beginning of the last century, child mortality was shockingly high. But death was something that happened as part of everyday life. Even though very distressing, it was regarded as normal. Families and the community dealt with it, because they knew what to do. There was a protocol around death and dying that we have lost.

These days people don't know what to do, or what is expected of them. I think one of the reasons is because we move around so much. We have lost our relationship with our local environment. It is now rare to die in the same community as our parents or grandparents, which means there is an alienation from other people, as well as from the landscape and the soil. But this isolation or aloneness also stops us from taking responsibility for what we are doing to the environment as well as to ourselves.[1]

So what happened to make us lose connection with the D-Word and, indeed, with the living world? To understand this, we need to take a journey back to medieval times.

Note

1   For those interested in how climate change is globally affecting human survival, T. S. Bennett's documentary film, *What a Way to Go: Life at the End of Empire*, is highly recommended.

CHAPTER 2

Days Gone By

Some facts and figures

During the 1400s, the Black Death was said to be responsible for over 75 million deaths worldwide. During the 1500s, smallpox was to become the most virulent killer.

Average life expectancy in medieval Britain was 20–30 years.

In Elizabethan days, almost one third of baptized babies died within the first year. Childbirth resulted in death for 2.5 per cent of mothers. Life expectancy increased after a child had reached 12, and was also influenced by wealth and social status.

End of the nineteenth century
Average life expectancy at the end of the nineteenth century in Western Europe was 20–37 years. In Victorian times, infant mortality was one in six, although towards the end of the era, life expectancy increased and infant mortality decreased, mainly due to improvements in sanitation.

American west frontier pioneers
Average life expectancy from birth is not known. It was thought to be between 45 and 50 years, although many lived into old age.

Early twentieth century
Average life expectancy in Western Europe was 30–40.

At the beginning of the 1900s, over 50 per cent of deaths occurred under the age of 45.

25 per cent of all deaths were due to infant mortality.

During the First World War, over 900,000 British died, including those from the Empire. It is estimated that between 8 and 12.5 million died worldwide.

The 1918 flu pandemic killed 250,000 in Britain alone. Between three and six per cent of the entire global population died.

During the Second World War, over 450,000 British soldiers and civilians died, with over 70 million dying worldwide.

Present day
For those born in 2009, in Western Europe, life expectancy for a female is 83 years, and for a male, 77 years.

Infant mortality has fallen to around one per cent.

Here follows a swift gallop through history about how we used to die. For a comprehensive understanding, *Death in England: An Illustrated History*[1] is highly recommended reading.

Before we depended on life-extending medicines, and before clean water and modern health care, death was a regular part of most ordinary people's everyday life. Death frequently visited families as a colourful cocktail of famine, drought, pestilence, infectious disease, plague, violence, war, injuries and, of course, childbirth and poor living conditions.

Most people in earlier days worked on the land and with animals, and there was a more fatalistic approach to dying, mainly because there was no choice. Without a welfare state, many lived in appalling poverty and deprivation with no means of obtaining medicine, pain relief or help, even if it had been available.

As well as being a natural transition, death was also a spiritual one. During the Middle Ages, Christianity in Europe increasingly influenced social and moral conduct, especially in the way people prepared to die at home. In the Christian faith, death had come to be regarded as spiritually dangerous, with evil fiends lying in wait to snatch away a sinful soul. So the manner in which a person conducted himself or herself during life and, crucially, prepared for death, was vital if they were to enter the heavenly afterlife.

A 'good death' saw people dying in their own bed, in full recognition of what was happening to them. It's worth remembering that almost everyone within older communities would already have personally experienced the death at home of a close relative – predominantly infants and mothers in childbirth – or would have been present shortly before, or at the moment when family members, neighbours and friends died.

It is essential not to romanticize the dying experience of olden times. Many died of horrible and painful infections and ailments without the possibility of medication or painkillers, but there was an expectation for young and old to learn how to identify failing health and fatal illnesses, and how long it might take to die. In fact, those who fell ill were actively encouraged to speak about prophetic dreams, visions, omens or auguries which might tell them they were dying. Family and friends were also expected to watch for changes, and to alert the priest when death was near so the last rites could be administered. So this recognition of impending death would provide a valuable time-frame in which the dying person could prepare for the anticipated entry into the afterlife.

Death was also regarded as a public event, where the dying could raise their social and moral status on their deathbed in the way they dispensed last-minute advice, bequeathed property and assets to family, friends and charities (particularly those associated with the Church), and drew up written or verbal confessions to seek pardon for their sins in order to be released from earthly misdeeds. Social historian Phillippe Ariès, author of *Western Attitudes Towards Death,* writes of the '. . . ritual organised by the dying person himself, who presided over it and knew its protocol'. As a result, no matter how awful it was going to be, the whole household, and the community, were ready to face what was coming.

Professor Allan Kellehear writes in *A Social History of Dying* that 'the end of a Good Life was nothing short of an ending which others would later describe as a Good Death – a death that met the criteria of the Good Life itself: it followed a gradual and predictable pattern, that involved others in an orderly exit to the next world'.

The medieval *Ars Moriendi*

Infectious diseases were rife during the Middle Ages. These diseases could kill people remarkably fast, and priests often could not reach the dying person in time. Therefore, lay people, such as relatives, had to take charge. To address this shortcoming, the Church created the *Ars Moriendi* (*Ars* – 'skill' or 'craft', *Moriendi* – 'of dying'). The original version was a text called *Tractatus* (or *Speculum*) *artis bene moriendi* ('Treatise on the art of dying well'), created in the early 1400s, and widely translated into most West European languages, including English.

A popular shorter version was produced in the Netherlands in the 1460s. William Caxton, the first person to introduce a printing press into England, printed his own *Arte and Crafte to Knowe Well to Dye* in 1490. Traditionally, the *Ars Moriendi* consisted of 11 wood-cuts (sometimes accompanied by text) illustrating a dying man's struggle to overcome the five great temptations – unbelief, despair, impatience, pride and avarice. These vices were symbolized by greedy devils surrounding the deathbed. On the opposing woodcut, a host of angels and other celestial forces rush to the dying man's side to support his struggle to overcome these ghastly evil forces. He resists angelic help five times, until the eleventh and final woodcut, which portrays the dying man finally accepting divine intervention and overcoming his sinful temptations.

The success of the *Ars Moriendi* lay in the simple illustrations acting as a kind of teaching aid, cutting across the social classes. Even the uneducated could reflect on the woodcuts and allow the images to convey the importance of redemption and true repentance as harbingers of their soul's salvation.

The mass production of the *Ars Moriendi* (made possible by the invention of the printing press) meant that most households in Europe had a copy. From an early age, children were encouraged to study the woodcuts and absorb the reality that one day they too would be forced to fight for entry into the afterlife. In the meantime, the woodcuts reminded them of the importance of living an honest, fulfilled life as a preparation for what was to come.

From home to hospital

By the sixteenth century, Papal Indulgences were being sold to ensure the remission of sins of those who had died and gone to purgatory. This was a place where souls were prepared for heaven by undergoing punishment for wrongdoings committed during their life. Relatives and friends could continue to influence the fate of the dead soul through prayers, purchasing indulgences, and paying for Mass to be said on their behalf, thus helping the departed soul to achieve a speedy passage through purgatory.

In 1517 in Germany, the monk Martin Luther rebelled. It is famously claimed that the devout Luther expressed his outrage against these indulgences by nailing his *95 Theses* to the door of the *Schlosskirche* (Castle Church) in Wittenberg on the River Elbe. His theses argued that the salvation of each man was a free gift from God and could only be secured through the forgiveness of Jesus as the Son of God. Therefore, Luther argued, the Bible – not the Church – was the only infallible authority on how a person might gain entry into the Kingdom of Heaven.

Luther gained a huge following, and his writings circulated widely, soon finding their way to England. Although King Henry VIII remained theologically close to Catholicism, he leant on Luther's reformation ideals to support his quest to divorce his Catholic wife, Catherine of Aragon, so he could marry Anne Boleyn – who, it is reported, expressed a keen interest in Luther's ideas.

Henry's Reformation and break with Rome began to change the way people spoke about death and dying, especially purgatory. During the subsequent reign of Henry's daughter, Elizabeth I, the whole idea of purgatory was swept away by Protestant faith, whose doctrine now declared that the fate of the soul was sealed at the moment of death. The living were no longer able to help the dead. Rather, the dying person was ultimately responsible for the purity of his or her own soul. However, this also meant that the way the person conducted himself or herself in life became much more of a focus.

Setting aside the controversy of the selling of indulgences, it could be argued that the Catholic belief – which embraced continuing links between the living and the dead – had benefits for both the dying and the bereaved, and that Protestant theology of the afterlife was much less benevolent. Nevertheless, a spiritual vacuum began to form, into which moved more secular understandings of the human condition.

French philosopher René Descartes' reintroduction of critical questioning during the 1700s gave rise to a much more rational approach to life and laid the foundation for the Age of Enlightenment. This led to an explosion of scientific exploration and the increasingly central role of medical practitioners in determining what happened in the sick room, and how much the dying person should know about what was going on.

In 1760, the English playwright and politician Richard Sheridan wrote: 'Very few people now die. Physicians take care to conceal people's danger from them. So they are carried off, properly speaking, without dying: that is to say, without being sensible of it.'

By the end of the eighteenth century, a highly moralistic code of conduct developed in England around the dying experience, particularly within the middle and upper classes. Courtesy, modesty and decorum were expected around the deathbed. To offset private grief, the bereaved built funereal monuments, modest ones for the less well-off, sometimes spectacularly elaborate ones for the wealthy.

The Victorians continued to move away from the spiritual or religious needs of those who were actually dying, to focus instead on elaborate funeral and mourning rites, which some historians argue were more to maintain social status and patriarchal power than to comfort the bereaved.

This coincided with the construction of a much-needed London sewer system to divert waste into the Thames Estuary rather than directly into the River Thames, which was so polluted that it had become a major health hazard. Other sewer systems were constructed throughout the country. This achievement, combined with better nutrition, public health and medical advancement, radically increased life expectancy.

Custom, language and expectation also developed around this time on how to behave after a person had died. Households would demonstrate their mourning with drawn curtains and clocks stopped at the moment of death. Mirrors would be covered to prevent the spirit of the dead person becoming trapped by their reflection. Women were expected to wear black mourning dress, sometimes for as long as two years. Men wore black suits. Children were also swathed in black, and even babies' clothing was trimmed with black ribbon as a mark of respect to the dead relative.

These very public displays of mourning continued until the First World War, when the country was forced to face death on a massive scale. It was quickly realized that an entire population clothed in black did little for public morale, nor did it encourage young men to sign up for military service. As war began in 1914, society magazines advocated the abandonment of mourning dress and, in 1918, at the war's end, as Kate Berridge reports in her book *Vigor Mortis,* the Easter sermon delivered from the pulpit of St Paul's Cathedral in London requested, for the well-being of the country, to 'cease this unseemly obsession with death'.

Death and dying became a private affair, spoken of in whispers or behind fluttering hands, and kept separate from the ritual of communal remembrance services. Although severely frowned upon by the establishment, many of the bereaved, particularly heartbroken wives, mothers, sisters and daughters, found solace in the rapid rise of spiritualism, through which they believed they could communicate with the departed spirits of their men-folk.

By the Second World War, there were significant advances in science and medicine. More than ever, the sick and injured turned to doctors to save their lives, with death increasingly taken out of the home and put into hospitals or care homes. In fact, it could be argued that it was during this time that medicine became the 'God of Death'. Doctors used medication not just to prolong life, but also, with the help of narcotics, to make the dying experience much less painful.

Within this focus on life – as opposed to death – arose a denial and ignorance of dying. Thankfully, witnessing death was no longer part of growing up for most children, but nor were they encouraged to know about it or speak about it. The Swiss psychiatrist, Dr Elisabeth Kübler-Ross, author of the ground-breaking book *On Death and Dying,* was one of the first medical professionals to write about her dismay at how death had become a 'dreaded and unspeakable issue to be avoided by any means possible in modern society'. Her concern was echoed by Ariès who wrote in the 1970s that 'a great silence has fallen on the subject of death in the twentieth century'.

Similar to Murray-Parkes, Professor Tony Walter, who now runs a Master's programme in 'Death and Society' at the University of Bath, argues that death is not necessarily a taboo subject, but that many people are ignorant of death. This is mainly, he says, because of a highly positive development: most people do not die until old age, most children do not grow up witnessing their siblings or parents die, so most enter adult life largely ignorant about death. In addition, with the end in much of Europe of nearly two millennia of Christianity as the dominant ideological culture, people can struggle to find words for what is happening beyond medical treatments.

> Those of us who are more secular have lost the language and the multi-sensory ritual that address the mystery of the things that we can't find words for, especially when someone is dying. Into this vacuum comes medicalization. Death is now hidden away in hospitals, hospices and nursing homes. So people latch on to medical language to try to make sense of what is happening.
>
> Even if you ask a non-medical question of a dying person or of relatives, they will usually answer with a medical account such as 'Well, the X-rays have shown the cancer has grown. It's leading to these other problems I am having.' They will talk in those terms because that's the only language available to them. However, this is different in Ireland and Northern Ireland, where there are still unbroken Catholic and Celtic traditions. Therefore, the language the Irish use around death and dying is a combination of spiritual and medical terminology.

Most people today, I suspect, would agree that the language used in doctors' surgeries and medical consulting rooms is usually restricted to a diagnosis of symptoms rather than underlying causes, or focuses on test results rather than the spiritual or emotional needs of the patient.

My own mother certainly turned into a catalogue of symptoms. She slowly disintegrated physically over several years until my father could no longer cope, and she was admitted into a local care home where her health continued to fade over a further three years. During this time she grew increasingly fearful of what was happening to her, but never dared to confront it, or herself. It played havoc with her peace of mind. I was with her when she died. It was truly awful to witness this gentle, kind, loving woman who had given birth to me, shouting out in confusion and fear before finally giving up her struggle to stay alive.

There was no *Ars Moriendi* for my mother. No art of dying well. Although a Christian, she had never found what might help to soothe her way. My consolation is knowing that I was there to hold her as she died, and to wish her well.

The media

So, if death is now kept absent from most people's personal experience, how do we actually learn about dying?

The short answer is, mostly, through the media. News bulletins, television soaps, films, newspapers and novels ply us with accounts usually of either over-romanticized deaths or overly horrific images of what it is like to die.

Now amplified by the internet, the media pump reports of disasters into our homes 24 hours a day. Gruesome images and harrowing stories are retold hour after hour. If we miss them on a multitude of satellite news channels, we can even download them onto our mobile phones. As a result, whether we like it or not, all of us are affected by what we see and read in the media.

Some say that high-profile media deaths, particularly when they happen in local neighbourhoods, can make people reassess their own lives, and often bring communities closer together. The murder of two girls by their school caretaker in Soham in 2002 was one such example. Subsequent media reports of, for instance, court appearances, coroner's reports or Government inquiries also help the public to make sense of what happened and, therefore, some kind of collective completion can occur.

However, sociologists have argued that this constant diet of violent or sudden death reduces our ability to talk about 'ordinary' death. Death happens to others, but not to us. Furthermore, since statistically most of us in the UK will live safely into our seventies and eighties, the news media's obsession with the harrowing is not an accurate account of how most of us are going to die. The result is the reinforcement of our sense of invincibility, for example, 'It won't happen to me because I don't live in an earthquake area or a war zone'; 'Well, I'm not in danger of dying from drought or famine'; or 'My own child is safe, so that's okay.'

Nevertheless, the media seem to love telling big stories about personal suffering and death. An example of this, of course, was how the life and death of Diana, Princess of Wales, was and still is making headline news. A more recent example concerns the *Big Brother* television celebrity Jade Goody, who declared her intention to die in the public eye. While I appreciated her determination to raise awareness of the importance of cervical cancer screening, and to provide financial support for her children, I don't think I was alone in experiencing a mixture of horrified ghoulishness and distaste at how her dying process was being portrayed.

Having been a nurse, I sincerely wondered how screaming tabloid headlines such as 'Jade's hospital hell', 'Jade's cancer agony' or 'Jade in the grip of terrifying hallucinations', really helped provide an accurate portrayal of what the dying experience is about. Yes, many terminally-ill people do suffer, but our palliative care service is highly developed in providing pain relief to help soothe those in physical and spiritual distress. I would have liked to have heard more about that.

Other celebrities, such as BBC radio presenter Gloria Hunniford and actress Sheila Hancock, have used the media in a far more measured way to tell their stories of how they coped with personal sorrow. Caron Keating, Hunniford's daughter, and Hancock's husband, the actor John Thaw, both died from cancer. The aim of these two autobiographies was to help others who have been similarly bereaved. Both books have been bestsellers.

However, when left to their own devices, the media do seem to be guilty of ignorance – or dare I say, laziness – in the way messages about death and dying are portrayed.

'The media have a lot to answer for when it comes to talking about death and dying', said a palliative care consultant. 'The media often talk about "cures" rather than treatment. But heart disease can't be "cured", although it can be treated with medication. And, often because most of us are so unprepared for someone to die, when he or she becomes ill, they are shipped into hospital to be "cured".' The consultant believes this 'feeds into a death-denial and death-defying culture'.

The news media's inaccurate use of language is reflected in the way most television soaps and dramas illustrate how we die. In most cases the dying person is seen lying prone on a hospital bed in a tidy, clean ward, with perhaps an intravenous drip or oxygen tube for company and a bleeping heart monitor to lend authenticity. He or she is surrounded by quietly weeping, loving relatives, one of whom will have turned up at the last minute for an emotional deathbed reconciliation. The dying person, at peace at last, breathes a final farewell, followed by the gentle closing of eyes. Fade to black and cue music.

It is understandable that grisly death scenes are unlikely to attract top ratings, so it would follow that scriptwriters tend to cobble together a one-size-fits-all deathbed scene which is acceptable for prime time viewing. But these unrealistic portrayals of death can be confusing, as experienced by Anne, a successful businesswoman in her mid-forties. 'I watch hospital soaps all the time. I love them. When people die, they look as if they have genuinely fallen asleep – their skin looks the same colour and they look at peace.' She continued:

> But when, for the first time, you see someone die, it's not like that at all. When my father died, his skin looked plastic. His face went yellow and leathery. It was nothing like him. I felt disappointed in myself that I was so unprepared for my Dad to look like this. Actually, I felt really resentful and let down by society.
>
> Another disappointment was the nursing staff. When someone dies on television, the head nurse is there to give the grieving relative a cup of tea and to sit with them and talk about how they are going to cope.
>
> Nothing like that happened. When my father died, I walked out of the hospital side room and told a nurse. It happened to be the 5th of November, so I was aware that this was going to be a busy night for the staff. Even so, I was shocked when she replied, 'Never mind, we'll get round to him when we can.' I went back into the side-room and told my mother. She decided it was best to leave, but I refused. I knew my father would never have left us like that. My mum told me not to be so stupid. It wouldn't make any difference to him if we stayed or not.
>
> At that point, the nurse came in and said, 'We won't get round to him for hours. It will probably be the morning staff who will put him in a shroud and take him down to the mortuary. He's just going to be lying here, so there's no point in staying.' I remember thinking, 'Hang on, that's my Dad. I am not disputing that's what you are going do, but do you need to be so matter-of-fact?' It would have been really nice if she expressed more compassion. Something like, 'We'll look after him. You go home and look after your Mum.' Yes, that was a real disappointment.

Another palliative care doctor agreed with Anne's perceptions.

> In films, the dying person is usually seen walking around quite happily. They have some kind of catastrophic illness and then abruptly die. But in real life, that's uncommon.
>
> Dying isn't an event, it's a process. So it can be hard for doctors to recognize when someone is actually going to die. When assessing patients, we have to take into consideration what the person used to do, and compare that with the help they now need to carry out everyday activities. It's about measuring the rate of their deterioration, taking into account all those remissions and plateaux that happen as well.
>
> Also, the majority of film deaths occur in a hospital setting with patients looking coiffured. In reality, when someone is very ill, they look fairly shocking. They are usually thin, or bloated, or yellow from jaundice, and can be unrecognizable from their former selves.

The media, and particularly soap operas, do provide a source of information about the D-Word. But unless we have an understanding of what *really* happens when someone approaches the end of life, we cannot prepare ourselves. This can add to an already stressful situation, often leaving us feeling alone, frightened and unsure of what to say or how to behave.

The following chapter looks realistically at the dying experience from a medical perspective, and provides advice and information on how health professionals broach the D-Word, and provide end-of-life care for the terminally ill and the elderly.

Note

1 *Death in England: An Illustrated History*, P. Jupp and Clare Gittings (eds), Rulgers University Press, 1999.

CHAPTER 3

Dying from a Medical perspective

Some medical information and terminology

Around 500,000 people die in England each year. Two-thirds are aged 75 and over.

Where we die
58 per cent in hospital
18 per cent at home
17 per cent in care homes
 4 per cent in a hospice
 3 per cent elsewhere

Hospices traditionally provide care for those with cancer. However, some hospices are now providing end-of-life care for those suffering from other forms of terminal illness.

Palliative care provides care to help relieve or soothe the symptoms of a disease or disorder where it is no longer curable.

Terminal illness is best defined as a life expectancy of six months or less, whether involving a malignancy or not. At this point the GP can sign a 'DS 1500' form for accelerated care benefits for the patient. The GP, district nurse or cancer care nurse will usually make sure this is done as soon as possible.

Chronic illness is a persistent or recurring illness which often results in disability and may shorten life expectancy.

A prognosis is the length of time a patient may have left to live. Sometimes referred to as a 'five-year survival rate', this refers to the statistical chance of the patient dying in the next five years (of anything). No one has a 100 per cent five-year survival expectancy. Life has its dangers. But someone with a terminal illness would have a low five-year life expectancy.

An 'Advanced Decision' in the UK or 'Advanced Directive' in Scotland (Living Will) otherwise called an 'Advanced Care Plan' is a legal document that stipulates, for example, whether you want to be resuscitated or, should you become seriously ill, what life-prolonging treatment you might wish for, or who you would like to be informed.

For a Living Will to be valid, you must be over 18 years old, and the document has to be signed, witnessed and dated while you are mentally capable. Hospices and care homes usually instigate an Advanced Care Plan when a patient or resident is first admitted, or you can download your own Living Will (see helpful advice, page 171). If so, it is advisable to give a copy to your GP or your solicitor, as well as to any next-of-kin who need to know your wishes should an emergency arise.

'Liverpool Care Pathway for End of Life Care'. The Liverpool Care Pathway is a form which provides guidance to carers on how to deliver the highest standard of care to the dying in the last few days and hours of life. This, or the equivalent, is now standard practice throughout the NHS and in most hospices and care homes.

An oncologist is a doctor who specializes in diagnosis and treatment of cancer. Most NHS hospitals have an oncology unit and a team of oncology nurses.

A palliative care consultant is a doctor who leads a specialist team in the provision and management of all patients with chronic and terminal illness. They are employed by the NHS and also work in hospices.

Macmillan nurses and palliative care clinical nurse specialists. Macmillan nurses are clinical nurse specialists in cancer and palliative care who are employed in a post that has been funded initially by Macmillan Cancer Relief and then by the NHS. They work in hospitals and in the community, but not usually within the private healthcare sector. To obtain the services of a Macmillan nurse or palliative care clinical nurse specialist, you must be referred by your GP, your hospital consultant, a district nurse or a hospital ward sister.

Marie Curie nurses are specially trained cancer or palliative care nurses, funded by the Marie Curie Cancer Care Charity. Their services are free to patients and their families, who are cared for by Marie Curie Hospices found throughout the UK.

Generally speaking, those who are dying from a terminal or chronic illness will spend most of their final year of life at home, even though many may spend periods of time in hospital or in a hospice. During these final months, most are cared for by relatives, friends and even neighbours, supported by healthcare professionals working within the community.

Those with cancer are usually supported by Macmillan nurses, arranged through the GP, who will come to the patient's home and liaise with the local hospice. The role of a hospice is to find ways of stabilizing patients so they can return home again, before they may need to be readmitted for final end-of-life care. When cancer patients choose to die at home, the hospice team do what they can to provide appropriate home care.

Those at home suffering from chronic illness, or who are becoming increasingly elderly, usually rely on relatives, friends and neighbours, plus support from their GP, District and Community nurses. Private nursing care is available at a cost. Home nursing can also be obtained through care agencies funded by the NHS, but the availability of these care agencies does vary from region to region. You would need to talk to your GP about different home-care options and who to contact. However, these groups of patients are more likely to be admitted into hospital or into care homes as their health deteriorates, or when they, or their carers, can no longer cope.

Admission into a hospital, hospice or care home can be a daunting and upsetting prospect for both patient and relative, especially when there is no information available about how the care system works, or indeed how or when to talk about the dying experience.

On the whole, my experience of the way my father, and my mother, were treated towards the end of their life by medical professionals was positive. But I was aware that being an ex-nurse helped in the way I was able to communicate with nurses and doctors, and so did my work as a researcher into end-of-life experiences.

Hospital staff caring for my father were clearly relieved when I spoke openly with them about his death. It lightened our conversations about his dying process, to the point when one charge nurse felt comfortable enough to risk a joke (there certainly is a place for humour) about the dying experience. I found his attitude healthy and reassuring. I also knew, because of the open relationship we had developed, he wouldn't lie to me.

Other interviewees for this book also had good experiences when they talked honestly to staff about their relative dying. One example was given by Janet, a 43-year-old policewoman.

> My mother had made her own decisions about her end-of-life care. But there came a point when, as a family, we were taken aside for what could have been a difficult conversation. The doctor was profoundly relieved when I helped her along by saying that I knew my mother was dying.

However, relatives and patients can be unnerved by the prospect of talking to medical staff. They may have spoken to a GP, but not to a palliative care consultant before, or even visited a hospital, hospice or care home. Consequently, they might not know what to expect or what a doctor may ask them.

To assist with this, I interviewed six medical professionals who specialize in providing end-of-life care in a variety of settings. Of course these six interviewees cannot represent the many thousands of medical professionals who work in palliative care. However, I hope the interviews will go a little way to provide relevant information and advice for a relative, friend or carer who doesn't know what to say or how to talk to medical professionals about death and dying.

The interviewees included a GP who talks about being the first port of call for those who are seriously ill; a consultant anaesthetist who works in an intensive care unit (ICU), who explains how he and his team make difficult end-of-life decisions; a palliative care consultant who expressed the need for clear communication about the D-Word; a palliative care clinical nurse specialist, based in a large hospital, who explores the best place for people to die; a hospice nurse who speaks of the importance of good listening skills; and a care-home carer who draws attention to the importance of talking and acting normally when the elderly are dying.

The GP: the first port of call

There are more than 30,000 GPs in England alone, and many of them work in urban, multi-cultural, and socially deprived areas which present their own end-of-life care issues. Adrian, a GP partner in a large general practice located in a rural part of southern England, reflects one particular perspective, but has been chosen because of the way he openly engages with death and dying. Patients across the UK may not always experience such intuitive awareness from their own GP.

The role of all GPs is to provide primary care for their patients. Therefore, when a patient's health is failing or under threat, the GP will arrange tests through an NHS hospital to establish what may be wrong. (Those patients with appropriate private health insurance will be seen and treated by their medical consultant.)

Tests could include blood, liver and bone marrow function, and perhaps a biopsy of a suspect lump. The test results provide the basis for a diagnosis and, when that is not clear, more tests will usually be recommended. So in some cases, there can be a time-lapse before the GP is able to assess what may be happening.

The GP will refer patients to medical consultants who specialize in a particular disease or part of the body, such as an oncologist for those with cancer, a heart specialist for those with heart complications, or surgeons for those who need operations. Patients may also ask their GP to arrange for a second opinion regarding their diagnosis.

Good communication skills, says Adrian, are essential when working in such a delicate area. But he acknowledges this can be tricky, particularly when English may not be the first language for either patient or doctor.

Bad news is emotionally traumatic to take on board. It can be impossible for the person to accept what they are being told. They may mishear information, or become confused by what is being said. Distraught relatives can also add to an already emotionally volatile situation by refusing to accept the diagnosis, demanding a second opinion, or expecting the GP to find a miracle cure.

Personally, I feel comfortable talking about dying, as long as the patient wants to. In most cases, some with a terminal illness will talk about it to a point, but it's almost like they are trying to protect their family from the reality of what is going to happen.

Seeing a GP is based around hope – hope of recovery, hope of a cure. Hope of managing the situation if nothing else. If I start talking about death it can equate to hopelessness unless the patient and doctor change gear together fairly smoothly. I usually listen for patient cues, such as 'How quickly am I going to get better?' or 'How serious is this?' Sometimes these cues can be very subtle – even non-verbal. I have to listen between the lines and respond accordingly.

I reply to their questions as clearly as possible. I explain about pain control and go through treatment options so they know this is an orderly process. But presumably one of the most important things for the patient to realize is that I have taken many others through this process. Dying and adjusting to death is familiar territory for me. I hope this gives them a kind of confidence.

But I'm not a counsellor or a spiritual mentor. I am a GP working under considerable time pressure. I try to use the 10–15-minute consultation to encourage them to tell me their thoughts, feelings, hopes and uncertainties, allowing the focus of the consultation to settle onto them as a person. I hope this also gives them the confidence to discuss what is happening with their families and friends – which I think is more important than talking to health professionals.

Adrian explained how, as the health of a patient declines, many GPs cultivate an awareness around financial issues that families will be forced to confront. There is a spiritual dimension to death, but there is also an economical one. Hospice and hospital care is not means-tested. Private care homes are, with the result that end-of-life care can become very expensive, particularly for the elderly. Apart from the emotional distress of possibly having to sell their home to meet these costs, it can cause conflict with relatives.

'When someone is reaching the end of life,' remarked Adrian candidly, 'extended family often start drifting in with a particular interest in the will.' He continued:

> I believe it's a priority to protect the patient for the interest of everyone. So I am very aware of the explicit and implicit implications of someone becoming terminally ill. Separate from talking through possible benefits for which the person may qualify, and raising awareness of the importance of having a will, this also includes whether the patient wants to be resuscitated and taken to hospital, or to die at home without further treatment.
>
> If I know they don't want to go to hospital, I can leave a special message with the out-of-hours emergency service, which goes to the Duty Doctor and to the ambulance service. This means that if there is a 999 call-out to the person in the early hours, they are not needlessly whipped off to casualty. When there is confusion or doubt about the best course of action, ambulance control will contact me to check. This provides legal protection to the patient and to the emergency staff. This is also why I think it is important for patients to make a Living Will.

Adrian emphasized the importance of providing the best possible care for his terminally ill patients.

> A patient's terminal care is such an important thing to get right. In our Practice, we have regular meetings with three community nurses, four GPs, and a couple of Macmillan nurses. This is a meeting we all make every effort to get to. Our aim is to provide continuity of care at a time when there is great emotional upheaval within the family. There's never a disagreement between our team, rather a pooling of information. It usually becomes obvious to us what needs doing and who should do it.

Things to think about

- The GP is normally the first port of call when someone's health begins to fail. If tests specify a terminal diagnosis, the GP generally only informs the patient if he or she wants to know.

- Irrespective of whether a terminally ill patient engages with their diagnosis, the GP will usually organize a team of health professionals to monitor the patient's progress and assess when they may require pain control. The aim is to provide cohesive end-of-life care, whether this happens in a hospital, a hospice, residential nursing care, or at home.

- The GP may discuss financial issues to see if the patient has made provision for their end-of-life care. This could open up further conversations about wills and Living Wills.

- The GP usually consults the next-of-kin when the patient becomes too ill to make end-of-life decisions.

- Ideally, if at any time you, as the next-of-kin, feel confused, frightened or unsure about what's happening, ask your GP questions. You may find that your GP is too busy to spend time with you. If so, ask to talk to the district nurse or a community nurse, or even the practice nurse.

- For free advice on making a will, talk to your local Citizens' Advice Bureau or look, for example, at the Make a Will website, www.makingawill.org.uk.

- For advice on how to construct your own Living Will (Advanced Decision) look, for example, on the Direct Government website, www.direct.gov.uk.

The intensive care anaesthetist: difficult end-of-life decisions

Richard has worked as an intensive care consultant anaesthetist for many years. He believes we have lost the language of dying,

In Victorian times, there was a 50 per cent infant mortality rate. It would be normal for three or four of your children to die. But now we are insulated against death. You can almost pretend it doesn't exist. You're never forced to think about it. This means that we only think about it if we get sick. But patients who arrive in ICU (Intensive Care Unit) are usually too sick to have a conversation, or to take on board what's going on. So there's no time for them to make plans.

Richard is constantly surprised how few families talk about what might happen when a close relative ends up on a life-support machine.

In my 20 years as a doctor, I have never yet looked after a patient who has made a Living Will (see page 20), nor someone gravely ill who has given enduring power of attorney to a next-of-kin. I find this extraordinary. We are all mortal and these end-of-life decisions are vital, whether you want to cling to life at all costs, or you wish to die in a more discrete way.

Actually, I think it is irresponsible not to consider the fact that one day you may become so ill that you are not able to express your wishes about how you want to end your life. It puts a huge burden onto relatives who are then expected to second-guess if you want life-prolonging treatment or not.

Richard works in a small unit, with just nine beds, and looks after approximately 600 patients a year. The patient group is varied, from the elderly who may have lived a full, healthy life, to 30-year-olds whose health is broken by, for example, substance abuse. On average, one or two patients are expected to die every week. Relatives have no other option but to face the reality that either the patient may die or, if they survive, their quality of life may well be impaired.

Richard calls this first meeting with relatives 'expectation management'. He believes patients and relatives need to be made aware of the reality, to counteract the unrealistic 'raising-of-Lazarus-like intensive care scenes' shown in television soaps. This kind of recovery, he explained, is very rare.

To ensure there is a continuity of message, the nurse looking after a patient is always present when the doctors talk to relatives. However, it is all too easy for distressed relatives to mishear or misunderstand information. One of the things we always ask is, 'What do you think is going to happen?'

It is essential they know that the patient is gravely ill and may die. It is equally important to have more than one family member present when we speak to them – particularly a relative who is not emotionally upset, or has a little distance from what's going on. It also helps us when relatives have a written list of questions about any concerns or queries they may have.

Once they understand the procedures we are suggesting, they are less fearful. This helps them to deal with the uncertainty of not having a guaranteed treatment routine. We can't provide certainty in ICU.

We can also glean from the relatives whether our patient is the kind of character who would want to continue treatment at all costs, or whether they would prefer not to.

However, families may not give accurate information about how the patient has been managing before their admission. Some relatives will say the patient has been well enough to look after the garden for the past year, when he or she clearly hasn't. Others will insist that the patient is still able to do the shopping. But dig a bit deeper, and you discover that the patient has been driven to the supermarket and left in the car while the daughter does the shopping. Likewise, when you ask if the patient can cope with stairs, 'Oh yes' will come the answer. But then you discover the patient uses a stair-lift!

There can come a time when a patient is so ill that ICU staff are forced to consider stopping life-prolonging treatment. Legally, no doctor can be forced or obliged to provide life-prolonging treatment if a point has been reached where either death is inevitable, death is being unnecessarily delayed, or the patient's quality of life will be so severely impaired that recovery is impossible.

Talking to relatives about stopping treatment is a delicate area.

Relatives can be difficult to talk to, especially if they haven't seen the patient for a while. For example, a son or daughter may have flown in from abroad. When they left the UK their mum was a sprightly 80-year-old. But being 85 is a different story. It's a huge shock to see her on a life-support machine.

These days, families are often a complex mixture of step-parents and children, divorced partners, estranged offspring and same-sex partnerships. It can be difficult for medical staff to work out who is the true next-of-kin. This can be extremely stressful, especially when families have fallen out.

Sadly, we have divided families who won't sit together in the same room. The best way to resolve this is for the family to nominate a spokesperson who is trusted, because in my experience, what you say to one side of the family will be heard completely differently by the other side.

Communication is made more difficult when, for example, relatives don't speak English. Others may have a drug or alcohol problem, or a mental health issue which means it is hard for them to take on board what is being said to them.

The decision to stop life-extending treatment lies with the ICU consultant, usually backed up with a second opinion.

Family have a right to be informed, but they must never be left with the idea that it's their decision how the patient is treated. It is not. This decision always lies with the medical team. But it's also important that relatives leave the hospital feeling that we did everything we could to help the patient.

The anaesthetist believes that end-of-life care is about adopting a common-sense attitude which has the best interest of the patient at heart. There is a time when the withdrawal of treatment is the only way forward. Most relatives will recognize this and, if someone doesn't, the team will take the time to explain why the decision is being made.

By the time we stop end-of-life treatment, it should not be a shock. Everyone can see that the patient is only being sustained by life-support machines such as a ventilator, or a kidney machine, or through large amounts of drugs to stabilize their blood pressure. Take all this away, and the patient would die within minutes or hours.

When the decision has been made, the ICU staff act quickly. Normally the patient will be put into a side room to give privacy to relatives. The patient is usually asleep when the anaesthetist turns the machinery off.

This responsibility comes with the territory of being a senior ICU anaesthetist. I would never ask anyone else in the team to do it. Once this has happened, we get rid of all the machinery and tubes so the person looks as normal as possible for their relatives to be with them as they die.

Turning off life-support takes an emotional toll on the team, but when someone dies in ICU we don't regard it as a failure. We know we have done everything possible to give the patient a dignified end of life, which has been made as pain-free as possible.

We also make sure the death certificate is completed quickly, alongside other necessary paperwork. This means families do not have to experience the distress of coming back to ICU the following day to sign forms. It's all part of doing a good job.

Things to think about

- It helps the ICU staff when you prepare a list of questions about any concerns you may have about the care of your dying relative, and it is important that you provide accurate information about your relative. Patient confidentially means that doctors will usually only talk to immediate next-of-kin.

- If you come from a large family, or a divided family, think about appointing a trusted spokesperson who is able to talk with the ICU staff and relay accurate information to everyone concerned. This is particularly important when your relative is too ill to be able to make their own end-of-life choices.

- If you come from a family that is fractured, or has problems communicating, it might be an idea to pause a moment, and to think what it might be like for the person who is dying. Perhaps it is the time to either set aside difficulties, or to find ways of resolving them.

- Responsibility for stopping life-prolonging treatment lies with the medical staff, *not relatives*. Once the decision has been made to stop treatment, the medical staff will act quickly. If you want to be present when machines are turned off, make sure you tell them. The medical team will do everything they can to ensure privacy and that all necessary paperwork is, as far as possible, completed on the day of death.

The palliative medicine consultant: clear communication

Mary works as a palliative medicine consultant in a busy teaching hospital in Yorkshire and is passionate about clear communication when it comes to talking about dying to terminally ill patients and their relatives.

Mary is particularly aware of how easy it is for patients – and relatives – to be confused by medical jargon.

> Medical staff are guilty of using euphemisms, which can cause misunderstanding. For example, 'shadow on the lung'. But what does this mean? Far better to say 'cancer' – and spell it out. The patient knows what they are dealing with and can begin to prepare for what is coming. Another example is when doctors talk about something being progressive. In lay terms the word progressive has positive connotations, but not in medical-speak when talking about progressive cancer or heart disease. Some nurses and doctors will describe a patient to their colleagues as 'poorly' or 'frail'. Again, what does that mean? It's important to say 'This person is dying.'
>
> The right use of language is essential to good end-of-life care. Nowadays, this is improving, but even in hospices I have heard nurses and doctors talking about someone 'passing away'. I always ask them to use the word 'dying'. It's our responsibility as professional carers to help the relatives to understand exactly what is happening.

With this in mind, at the first meeting with a patient, Mary asks three questions to glean how much the person knows about their diagnosis: 'What do you think is happening?', 'What have you been told already?' and 'Do you want to have further information?'

> Depending on how the patient answers, I can determine whether they are willing to engage with the severity of their illness or not. But I am also aware that patients often know they are dying and will volunteer this information by making a comment such as, 'It's not looking too good.' Others make it equally clear that, although they know they are not well, they do not want to go into further details.

Mary admits it can be complex, rather like embarking on a fact-finding mission, to identify when someone is actually dying.

> Unless you've seen them regularly, you don't know how quickly things have been changing. But once people actively start to die, regardless of their diagnosis, there are certain patterns I look for.
>
> They take to their beds, spending at least half their time there, or find it increasingly difficult to get out of bed or the chair where they are most comfortable. They are spending most of their time asleep and their level of consciousness starts to drift. They have difficulty taking in fluids and food – or not wanting to. They have difficulty taking tablets or medication.

In 17 years of working in palliative care, Mary has seldom experienced families broaching the possibility of stopping life-prolonging treatment. She thinks one reason could be that some people genuinely believe life can go on for ever, which causes her concern.

> The problem is that death is not optional. But I sometimes get the feeling that patients and relatives believe that it is.

Another reason, Mary believes, could be a lack of clarity from some doctors when no more can be done for the dying person.

> Surgeons, for example, have to be very incisive and decisive. That's why they are good at their job. But when they realize they can't do any more, they often end up saying nothing rather than getting into the D-Word conversation. This can be confusing for patients. Of course it's a good thing to involve a doctor who is more skilled in communicating such complex issues, but I think we need to get into the situation when every doctor and nurse is able to talk openly to patients about the possibility of dying – assuming that the patient wants to know.

As a palliative medicine consultant, Mary is particularly aware of the importance of clear language when explaining end-of-life care, especially, for example, when it comes to fluid intake. She says that families are often under the false impression that the patient will starve to death or die of thirst if fluids are stopped.

This is not so. The patient does not die of thirst – they are dying of their disease, be this cancer or something else. I always explain that continuing with fluids can make it worse – it can, for example, cause water retention, incontinence or make breathing very difficult. That can cause considerable distress to relatives and, of course, to the patient. The most important thing is to explain that we are here to keep the patient's pain and breathing under control so he or she is as comfortable as possible.

Mary stresses the importance of plain language when it comes to talking to relatives about stopping life-prolonging treatment. She confirms how important it is to understand that responsibility for this lies with the medical staff, not with relatives. But she knows it is easy for relatives to misinterpret what is being said at the time.

I know of one doctor who thought he had been very clear with the wife of someone who was dying. The doctor told the wife that when her husband's heart stopped, the medical staff would not be starting it again. 'Is that all right with you?', he asked in passing. A few weeks later the doctor met the wife again. She told him, 'That was the hardest decision I have ever had to make.' The doctor was taken aback and asked what she was referring to. The wife replied, 'When you said if it was all right with me, not to have his heart started again.' The doctor was shocked that the wife should have mistakenly assumed liability for this.

Things to think about

- The medical team should ask the dying person questions to understand whether they want to be informed of their diagnosis or prognosis. It is up to the patient to decide how much information they receive.

- There are certain patterns that a dying person will adopt as they near their end of life. Knowing what to expect can help

relatives to prepare for this. However, it is *not* the responsibility
of relatives to make decisions about ending life-prolonging
treatments. If you feel guilty or upset about anything to do with
this, talk to the doctors and nurses.

• If you don't understand what is being said to you, ask for clar-
ification – especially if you are confused by medical jargon.

The palliative care clinical nurse specialist: planning the best place in which to die

'I am often one of the first to name it when someone is dying,' said
Sandra, a palliative care clinical nurse specialist who works in central
London. She manages a large multi-cultural caseload of terminally ill
patients and assesses their medical needs.

Many of her patients are admitted into hospital when their illness
is in an advanced state. However, Sandra says, doctors may not con-
firm that a patient is dying until a few weeks or days before it happens, if at all. Medical discussions are more likely to focus on when
a patient is no longer responding to treatment.

A major part of my role is to recognize that the patient is dying, and
to make my opinion known to the rest of team. This means I can then
start to have important conversations with the patient about their
end-of-life care. This could include anything from speaking to the
team about the possibility of withdrawing end-of-life treatments, to
arranging for the patient to go home to die.

Sandra spent many years working as a palliative care nurse in various hospices and in the community as part of a palliative care team.
However, working as a clinical nurse specialist (a qualified nurse
who has had additional training in medical assessment) means she is
able to draw up an end-of-life care plan to suit each patient.

When making major life-and-death decisions with patients, relatives
and doctors, it is vital to have medical training to know what you are
dealing with. Patients need to know you are an expert to feel safe.

And, for me, these hard-nosed medical decisions allow me to be cre-
ative and flexible in the way I can support the patient.

Although she is proud of how palliative care is provided in the UK,
Sandra realizes that the majority of us die in hospitals, hospices and
care homes, where the medicalization of death has overtaken spiritual values. This, she believes, means few us have the opportunity to
learn how to prepare for death, emotionally or spiritually.

I always ask patients at some point during my discussions with them,
if they have any spiritual beliefs – or if they have thoughts about the
afterlife. They will often say, with amazement, that I am the first
person to ask this kind of question. They are grateful too because it
gives them a chance to think about any beliefs they may have.

Sandra is well aware that all her patients have very individual needs.
She also says that some may want to know about their diagnosis and
prognosis, others do not. It is Sandra's job to find this out.

The first thing I do is to encourage the patient to tell me their story.
What brought them into hospital? I then ask them to tell me what
the doctors have said and what they understand by this. For example,
a patient may say, 'Well, the doctor said they hoped I might be able
to walk after the chemotherapy.'
    If I know they are not going to walk again, and it is obvious they
are not responding to treatment, I will gently broach the subject to
find out if they want further information. I think this gives the choice
back to the patient. I am aware that some may be outraged to be
told they are not going to get better.

Sandra respects that some patients do not want to engage with the
reality that they are dying. She is also aware that this may change
over time, particularly as the patient's health continues to fail.

Often a patient will say, for example, 'I am worried I am not going to
walk again.' I will respond by asking them how they are seeing their
future. Some will say, 'Well, I am waiting for the man upstairs to call
me, I don't think I have got long.'
    Once they use language like this, it becomes much easier for me.

I know they are admitting to themselves they are dying, and I can begin to open up conversations with them about where they want to die, and how they would like to sort out their affairs.

Once a patient is willing to talk about what's happening, their questions usually revolve around how long they have left to live, how to tell their family they are dying, and whether suggested treatments will help them to live longer, or will control their symptoms.

They are usually anxious to know whether they will be in hospital for most of the time or at home. If they want to go home, I talk to them about the possibility of getting extra help through the NHS and how much it's going to cost if this funding isn't available.

However, Sandra's multi-cultural caseload can present further challenges. A large proportion of her patients do not have English as their mother tongue, so it is essential for her to constantly check whether the patient understands what she is saying. She regards herself as a stage manager in the way she facilitates opportunities for patients to talk – if they want to – about their dying process.

Death is a natural, normal part of life. Facing it and talking about it gives the patient permission to make informed decisions about what they want, and a rite of passage to say 'I am dying'. Once this is stated clearly, everyone concerned can prepare for what is to come. But if you have never spoken openly about things that matter to you during your life, it is unlikely to happen at the end of your life either. Relatives respond differently too. For instance, one relative may not want to acknowledge that the person is dying, while another one will be rushing off to find the prepayment funeral plan.

Sandra is always relieved when someone has thought through what might happen when they die.

I am very glad when a patient has made a will and thought about legal arrangements, such as signing over rental agreements or how they are going to finance their funeral. It's difficult for families when, on top of everything else, they are left with a financial mess to deal with.

To help patients to make informed choices about their end-of-life care, Sandra discusses the Department of Health's 'End-of-life Care Strategy' (published July 2008). One of its aims is to educate the public about the importance of making an advanced care plan or Living Will (see page 20). If a patient wants to die at home, Sandra does everything she can to make this possible.

However, she also talks through the logistics with spouses or other relatives. For example, the patient may live in a high-rise flat which makes access difficult. Or their spouse may be elderly or suffering from ill-health themselves, which makes it difficult to provide the kind of care the patient needs. If a daughter or son becomes involved, they may need to take extended time off work or arrange for child-care. All this can be very stressful.

When a patient is determined to go home, I like to know that there is someone there who can help them to eat, or to lift and turn them regularly. I also talk through the implications with relatives, for example, of being faced with seeing mum or dad naked – perhaps for the first time ever – or losing control of their bowels. All these things need to be thought about carefully. It can become quite complex and exhausting for relatives, no matter how close they are to the dying person. So dying at home is not ideal for everyone.

Things to think about

- Essentially, home may not always be the best place for your relative to die, especially if they require specialized nursing care. Consequently, it is important not to feel guilty if, for example, the dying person cannot be taken home or stay there.

- The palliative care clinical nurse specialist (or Macmillan nurse) is an important member of the NHS palliative care team. Part of his or her job is to assess if the patient knows – or wants to know – about their diagnosis or prognosis. Patients can only be referred through their GP, or the hospital team.

- If the patient wants to know what is happening to them, the palliative care clinical nurse specialist will help patients make informed choices about their end-of-life care preferences, such as where they would like to die and whether the patient has thought of financial and legal issues that may need attention. As such, they act as medical and pastoral strategists, working out how the needs of the patient can be realistically met within the NHS system.

- As next-of-kin, if you are confused or anxious about any aspect of end-of-life care your relative is receiving, or the logistics of caring for your relative at home, ask to talk to the Clinical Nurse Specialist through your GP or hospital team.

The hospice nurse: the importance of listening

In 1967, Dame Cicely Saunders at St Christopher's Hospice in London, started the hospice movement to care for people dying from cancer. Some hospices receive funding from the government or NHS. However, the majority hold charitable status and rely heavily on local support and community fund-raising events. Many auxiliary hospice workers are volunteers.

The hospice philosophy centres on the right of a terminally-ill person to spend as much time as they can at home. Hospice care provides medical, social, emotional and spiritual care to support their patients. The majority of hospice patients have cancer, although others may have chronic illnesses such as HIV/AIDS or heart and lung disease. Patients can be any age, race or hold different religious or spiritual beliefs.

Hospice nurses are usually qualified nurses who have chosen to work in hospice care. These nurses carry out traditional nursing care duties such as recording symptoms, administering medication and working closely with doctors in order to minimize physical pain and discomfort and to make the last few weeks and days for patients as comfortable as possible.

An equally important role for nursing staff is to provide emotional support to those in their care, in the knowledge that they are dying. Therefore, hospice nurses often spend time providing home care, talking to relatives or liaising between families and medical professionals. They may also work alongside social workers and other carers.

Most hospices have a day centre facility which helps staff to build up a rapport with patients in the early stage of their illness (and to give carers a break).

Jo is a palliative care nurse who has worked 'hands on' in hospices for many years. She is very aware that the physical nature of death can make it hard for relatives and friends to witness.

No one knows what dying is really going to feel like, either physically or emotionally – or when it is going to happen. And there's a lot to dying which is beyond our control and certainly beyond our understanding. So of course the thought of it can become terrifying. But I wish we could talk more openly about death.

Jo believes that, unless we are prepared to face our own mortality in a positive sense, it is very difficult for any of us to accept and plan for our death.

When patients are not willing to think or talk about their terminal illness, they can often feel punished or singled out in some way. I find this really sad.

Their isolation and distress also means that patients tend to create unrealistic judgements of other people's lives – especially when it comes to those who care for them. For instance, they may believe that doctors and nurses are invincible, or we are immune from the same life problems as they have. When I think this is happening, I will often drop comments into a conversation I am having with the patient such as, 'When it's my turn to face this . . .'

I want them to know that I am not impervious to dying, or that one day I might also confront what they are going through. I think this helps them to realize they are not alone.

One of the most important aspects of Jo's role as a hospice nurse is to enable patients – if they want to – to talk about how they are feeling about their illness and approaching death.

> Of course we must never force anyone to talk if they don't want to. But I do believe that, as nurses working in palliative care, we need to strive to create an environment where patients can feel in control and are able to safely express what they want to. However, we need to respect that these patients must be allowed to guide the level of conversation they wish to have.
>
> Some patients want to talk quite openly, others are much more guarded. So it's being sensitive to what patients need in any given moment, and perhaps prompt an opportunity for them to talk by asking simple questions such as, 'How are you feeling today?'

Jo is aware that these important conversations can happen spontaneously. Patients tend to choose who they want to talk to and will often wait until they feel safe enough to open up a conversation. This may be in more intimate moments, for instance, when they are being helped with their meals or while washing.

> Not so long ago, I was taken aback by an elderly lady we were caring for. She was clearly struggling to come to terms with her admission into the hospice and not really willing to communicate with either the staff or other patients.
>
> While I was helping her to bathe, she suddenly opened up and told me about the frustration and anger she felt about her life and her disappointment at wasted opportunities.
>
> It was as though she needed the warmth of the water and the quiet of the bathroom to help her relax enough to tell me what was going on for her. Her bath took over an hour. But it was worth it. During our conversation I discovered she loved a certain genre of stories. But because of failing eyesight, she couldn't read any more. So we organized some audio-tapes read by her favourite actors. It made a huge difference to her and the way in which she began to communicate with us all.

Although Jo has experienced many similar situations, she has also had conversations where she has felt powerless to help; particularly when speaking with relatives.

> It's easy to feel inadequate when families are overwhelmed with grief. At times like this, I have to cling to the fact that at least they are not alone. All the staff are here to support them, and many of us have been through the same thing.
>
> From my own experience of my father dying of heart disease 15 years ago, I know how hard it is at first. But life – in its miraculous way – still goes on. And the pain you feel, to a greater or lesser extent, just becomes part of you.

Jo considers the UK hospice movement to be one of the best in the world. But there is always room for improvement.

> I like how the Government is acknowledging that palliative care services need to be available to all – not just to cancer patients – and that people need to be provided with the option to die at home.

However, the most important support Jo receives is through the teamwork she enjoys with her colleagues.

> I couldn't survive as a hospice nurse for very long without the support of the people I work with – all of whom I consider as friends. I think it's true that nurses in general have a very black sense of humour. Perhaps palliative care nurses have an even blacker one. Patients love it when they hear us laughing. It makes them feel safe and supported.
>
> And let's face it, it's good to blow a big fat raspberry to death every now and again!

Things to think about

- Anyone who is diagnosed with a terminal illness is eligible for hospice care. Many hospices provide free care, but talk to your GP or local hospice about possible costs. There are also private health insurance companies who deal with terminal illness. Talk to your GP or check on the internet.

- Most hospices are short-stay. They work towards stabilizing terminally-ill patients to enable them to spend quality time at home before being re-admitted, if required, for the final weeks or days of life. Most hospices have a day centre for people living at home and offer home care. The hospice will continue to support a patient whether they choose to go home, are admitted into hospital for further treatment, or maybe transferred to a care home.

- When a patient is admitted into a hospice, staff understand that this can be new territory for many relatives and friends. So ask any question you want – big, small, practical, spiritual. Learning about the dying process means that all questions are relevant. The staff will be happy to help and support you. Often hospices have special rooms set aside for relatives to stay overnight.

- For more information on hospice care, go to www.terminal illness.co.uk/hospice-care. And keep asking questions of your hospice nurse – even if it's only to know what they may think might happen next to the dying person.

The care-home carer: importance of acting normally

Care homes are very different from hospices. They provide long-term care mainly for elderly residents and are either funded through the NHS or privately owned by individuals, company groups or by large healthcare organizations such as BUPA.

Care homes are regulated by the Commission for Social Care Inspection (CSCI), which is responsible for monitoring the standards of most private, voluntary and local council care services.

CSCI inspects all registered care homes to make sure they meet National Minimum Standards, which are set by the Department of Health. The CSCI only registers care homes if they meet these standards. There is more information on the Directgov website: www.direct.gov.uk.

There are more than 21,500 registered care homes in the UK, including residential homes and nursing homes. A growing number of care homes now tend to take residents both with and without nursing care needs. Private care homes are run as viable businesses so the quality of care can vary. It's important to talk through any choices and decisions with your GP and/or your family. GPs can't ethically recommend any particular home, though they will discuss options. It's usually Social Services who decide on the level of care required.

Care homes can be expensive, so considerable planning and thought may need to be put towards ways of meeting ongoing fees. Sometimes, after a financial assessment, local councils can contribute towards costs.

Most nursing care homes are staffed by qualified nurses, nursing assistants and auxiliaries, led by a matron. The majority of care homes follow the Government's end-of-life care strategy and assess the individual needs of each resident when they first arrive. Residential homes that do not offer 'nursing beds' may have no staff with nursing training. So, it is important to find out, as best you can, how confident any residential home is with providing end-of-life care. Many are very good if properly supported by the community nursing staff.

Natalie is the deputy matron of a care home, which is part of a large privately owned health-care group. She recognizes a marked difference between working with terminal illness and looking after elderly residents who may have years to live; and also how difficult it can be, even for experienced carers such as herself, to talk about death and dying.

> You don't know when a resident is going to die, so we often find it difficult to bring this up when residents first come in. For example, when a resident is admitted, all the questions in the initial Assessment Sheet will be filled out – from mobility, to what kind of glasses the resident wears. But not the bit about their end-of-life care. It just feels crass to go into it as soon as they step over the threshold.

I think it would be much easier if they were a terminally-ill patient. Everyone knows what's happening. But with an elderly person, they might not want to face the fact that they have come here to die, or they may be here for many years. In their minds they have come into the home because they can no longer cope at home. That's very different.

Natalie will often turn to next-of-kin when it comes to addressing end-of-life issues.

We normally start the conversation with a relative by asking, for example, if anything were to happen to their mother or father, what would they like to happen – who would they like us to call? That clears up any misunderstandings and we have indirectly prepared them that, at some point in the future, the resident is going to die.

However, Natalie is aware that many relatives are not willing to face the inevitable. This impacts on how her staff are able to talk about it too. Natalie admits that all too often death becomes the elephant in the room.

I suppose we don't like to admit it's going to happen because it makes us face our own mortality. But residents do know when they are reaching the end of life. Personally, if I knew I was dying, I would find it very difficult if no one asked me what I wanted, or if I didn't know what was going to happen to me.

There are many occasions when the care-home staff are asked by relatives not to tell the resident they are dying. Professionally, it's part of Natalie's job to respect the wishes of relatives. However, she often finds it difficult, especially when it conflicts with her duty of care to the resident.

It definitely affects the morale of the staff. But we have to go with the family's wishes. Not so long ago we had a man in his sixties admitted with a terminal illness, but his family did not want him to know he was dying. His wife came in every afternoon to sit with him and care for him. She was incredibly attentive. But nothing was mentioned about the fact that he was dying. Personally, I would have liked to have known what the resident wanted himself, but I knew that would have been going against her wishes.

Natalie believes some relatives have no idea how to behave around the dying, which is why they tend to negate the feelings of the dying person.

> The awful thing is the hushed voices and the whispering. Relatives go all quiet and creep around the room in an unnatural way. They wouldn't do this in ordinary life. So why do it now? I think it's probably about putting up an appearance, because people don't want to be perceived as uncaring or inappropriate. But that's exactly what's happening. And I can imagine some residents thinking, 'What on earth are they doing?'

Natalie admits that many of her staff don't know how to respond to residents who want to talk about dying. But a lack of honesty in the way in which death and dying is spoken about has consequences.

> I'm sad to say that the usual response is, 'Cheer up – don't think like that. Look, you've got some lunch here.' I've done it myself. It must be awful for the person. You know you are not answering their questions or giving them what they want. It's more serious too because it undermines your relationship with them. They know you have lied to them. So it's about learning to be respectful to those who want to know, and those who do not.

Natalie also thinks that the media get it wrong: the number of pour-your-heart-out television documentaries is out of balance compared with the reality of everyday dying, especially when it comes to the elderly.

> I know dying is never going to be a cause of celebration, but it's important to get rid of the gloomy stigma that is attached to it. In some cases dying is a relief for the resident and their relatives. Yes, families are sad. Yes, they grieve. But they do get on with life. You have to.

This is evident in the way in which much of Natalie's work is concerned with supporting relatives after a resident has died.

> In these moments, relatives don't want to be told what to do, or what *you* think. They aren't looking for answers, they just want to be heard; for someone to witness how *they* are feeling – which could be anything – sad, angry, guilty or relieved.
>
> Because of my personal experience of grief, I understand the importance of allowing relatives to say what they want to say, without me stepping in with platitudes or euphemisms like 'passed on'. So I never lessen what they are going through. It's an important part of their grieving process.

Natalie's work has made her face the importance of talking about her own death to her family.

> I've made a will. I want everyone to know what I want. When the time is right, I will also talk to my son. He's only four, but he will be forced to face death at some point in his life, like us all. But I don't want him to experience what happened to me when my grandmother died. I had to cope with the shock of seeing my father cry, made worse when I was stopped from going to her funeral. That's always been a regret for me.
>
> I just wish that people – and I know that does include me – would stop hedging around all this. We have lost respect for the police, teachers, old people, politicians, even our banking system, but not death. It's inevitable that we are all going to die. We don't know when or how, but it is going to happen. We need to be ready for it.

Things to think about

- Care homes cater for long-term elderly residents or those who are no longer able to cope on their own. However, family members can feel guilty for putting their relatives into a care home, especially when the person has been fiercely independent. Consequently, visits may become emotionally demanding and stressful for both resident and relative.

- Care homes are either privately owned or funded by the NHS. This means that quality of care can vary. Those registered with CSCI have met National Minimum Standards.

- Long-term care is expensive, so it is important to consider financial implications and to make sure that fees can be met over the years, or that financial assessments are made to enable local councils to provide financial support.

- Most care homes will automatically assess the needs of the resident when they are first admitted. This includes filling out an Advance Care Plan, including any end-of-life care wishes. It is particularly important for staff to know who to contact when the resident falls ill or dies. If the resident is unwilling or unable to talk about this, or the staff feel awkward addressing it with the resident, next-of-kin are usually consulted.

- Although some residents may prefer not to discuss end-of-life issues, it is important that staff and family members are aware that their own awkwardness can deny the resident an opportunity to express what he or she would like to happen.

- Care home staff usually encourage regular visits from relatives, and may want to consult them on continuing medical treatment, especially when the resident's health is failing.

- When a resident's health fails or reaches a crisis they will often be taken to hospital, and may die there. If the resident does not want this to happen, it must be stipulated on their Advanced Care Plan, and their GP informed.

- Care homes do not usually provide rooms for relatives to stay overnight, but are normally happy for next-of-kin to spend as much time as possible with the dying resident – although this does vary in different care homes.

- If you are concerned about the care your elderly relative is receiving, talk to your GP.

We have considered the practicalities of talking about death and dying from the medical perspective. The other side of this is a more spiritual approach to dying. However, because we live in an increasingly secular society, many of us are unsure of who to talk to, or what is appropriate when seeking pastoral care. The next chapter looks at these questions and explores how different approaches to faith can help in coming to terms with the dying experience.

CHAPTER 4

Faith May Help

Some information

After centuries as an essentially Christian society, the UK is rapidly becoming a multi-faith society.

There is an active inter-faith network in the UK, founded in 1987 to promote good relations between people of different religious and spiritual beliefs. Communities include Baha'i, Buddhist, Christian, Hindu, Jain, Jewish, Muslim, Sikh and Zoroastrian, as well as national and local inter-faith bodies, academic and educational institutions concerned with inter-faith issues.

Most hospitals have resident Christian chaplains and a chaplaincy office. They will be happy to see patients and relatives whether they have a religious belief or not. Hospital chaplains can also arrange for other faith denominations to visit.

Most hospices and care homes have an inter-faith policy and will arrange for different faith denominations to visit patients and talk to relatives when requested. The local vicar and/or chaplain will also play a role in providing care and support to staff.

Those patients who remain at home may want to organize their own pastoral support.

If appropriate, inform your local vicar or faith leader of what is happening. They will be pleased to be of help to both patient and family, whether in hospital, hospice, care home or at home.

I am not a religious person, but during the time my father was dying in hospital I was deeply moved by the care and compassion he and I received from the hospital chaplain, and from his local parish priest.

As soon as my father had been settled into a side-room of a main ward where I knew he was going to die, I felt compelled to go in search of the hospital chaplain. I wasn't sure what she could do, but I felt it was an important gesture for my father because he was of the old school – I don't honestly think he was particularly devout, but I knew that his parish church, and the relationship he had with his vicar, meant a lot to him, especially after my mother died. Before it had become more difficult for him to walk, he had been part of the Church's cleaning crew, made up of local ladies of a certain age. He loved their company and especially the gossip.

The hospital chaplain wasn't there, so I left a message and returned to sit beside my father. A short time later a smiley-faced volunteer chaplaincy visitor appeared at the door to say the chaplain would be calling by later, but would I like prayers to be said in the meantime? I found this a very comforting and kind gesture and was touched when she moved closer to my father, quietly opened her prayer book and prayed for him.

Later in the morning, my father's vicar unexpectedly popped in. After a few minutes he shyly withdrew from his pocket a small pot of sacred oil. 'Could I anoint your father?' he asked tentatively, holding forth the pot. At first I was taken aback by his gesture. Not because I didn't want him to do it, it was just that I had never experienced this ritual before.

With some apprehension, I stood aside while the vicar carefully dipped his forefinger into the oil and leant over my father to draw a cross on his forehead and give him the last rites. This was one of the most moving acts I have ever witnessed, made more poignant because of my father's inability to respond. But I knew he felt it. I knew he had been given the freedom to die.

Later on, the hospital chaplain appeared. Her kindness and compassion towards my father was extraordinary. She took his hand and spoke to him as if he was his normal self and asked him if there was anything that was troubling him or keeping him from dying at peace. Her question brought a lump to my throat, so I left the two of them to it. I have no idea what went on while she was with my father, but

I knew that some kind of magic was taking place. Even though he was barely conscious, her presence was giving him something that neither the nursing staff nor I could.

During the six days it took for my father to die, she came every day to see him and to say prayers by his bedside in the evening when I wasn't there. Her being there provided my father – and me – with a spiritual comfort that was priceless.

Looking back, I wish my mother had received the same quality of spiritual care that my father had. I now regret not asking for her vicar to provide her with the last rites. Perhaps it would have helped to calm the distress that caused her to cry out right until the end.

I am not alone in experiencing the end-of-life being more than a physical closing down of the body's system. Something else happens too, which can't be pathologized. This is illustrated by the story of Victoria, a 42-year-old mother of three teenagers. When we spoke, she had been recently diagnosed with terminal cancer.

> When you are faced with the prospect of dying, it changes your whole perspective. I think you are 'pressed into God', which takes you into a more spiritual space. A place of healing. It also makes you question your attitudes and what motivates and matters to you.
>
> I feel very thankful that I have such a strong Christian faith. I don't know how people cope when they haven't got a faith. It makes me think of black spaces and oblivion. But my faith gives me peace and trust.
>
> My faith also helped me to make my own decisions about how I wanted to tackle this diagnosis. I'm a trained psychiatric nurse, so I know a lot about medical procedures. I have also read a lot about breast cancer. So, rather than going down the normal medical route after surgery, I decided not to have further treatment
>
> Naturally I think of what's going on in my body. Getting a terminal diagnosis is an extraordinary experience. You go to bed with it and you wake up with it. But it's made me want to prepare myself and to really look at my life – what I need to change or anything I need to complete. I find that prayer is very helpful with this. It takes me to a spiritual place where I can find peace, direction and inner knowledge. My illness has also made me much more compassionate towards other people who are suffering or sick. But perhaps a little impatient with those who complain about the more superficial things in life.

I like the fact I have taken responsibility for myself. Yes, at times I do become fearful. But when this happens I turn to prayer, so I am willing to face the consequences rather than letting other people make decisions for me. I don't feel greedy for life. I just want to do the best I can for my family, friends and church for as long as I can. I have three children and I feel I have a lot more to give to their lives. But if it wasn't for them, and those in my life whom I love, the prospect of dying wouldn't bother me so much. My belief in the afterlife means, for me, that dying is like arriving at the most perfect destination and coming home all at the same time.

Elisabeth Kübler-Ross was one of the first doctors to talk about the importance of meeting the spiritual or religious needs of the dying. Nonetheless, we are often unsure how to provide spiritual care to the dying, or even how to recognize what the dying person may need in the way of spiritual support.

I am not suggesting for one moment that the dying should be forced into religious or spiritual end-of-life rites and rituals. Many people die firm non-believers, and that must be respected. But evidence suggests that, similar to Victoria's experience, the nearer we get to the end of our life, the more questions can arise about the meaning and purpose of our existence. So don't be afraid to knock on the hospital chaplain's door, or to ask for pastoral support to be organized by hospice and care-home staff.

Because of the vast number of religious and spiritual beliefs, it's impossible to explore every approach to the dying experience. So for the purposes of this book, I have focused on five different religions practised in the UK, which I hope will provide a broad overview.

There follows personal interviews from Christian, Muslim, Jewish, Buddhist and Hindu perspectives. I hope they will go a little way to provide some understanding of how different religious beliefs look at end-of-life issues, and how each story, in its own way, may help those accompanying the dying to feel more comfortable about asking for spiritual or religious support for them and their dying relative, whether believer, agnostic or atheist.

The Bishop: the Easter story

Bishop Michael of Gloucester

As a society, I don't think we are as uptight in the way we talk about dying as we were a few years ago. In the life of the Church, we talk about dying a lot. But not necessarily in a personal sense. The focus is on the death of Christ, particularly during Easter's Holy Week.

Holy Week provides us with an opportunity to connect with the emotional suffering Christ went through leading up to his death. This can help when we too are faced with similar suffering, prompted by our own fear of death. When we reflect on Christ's story and are willing to talk about his death and resurrection – especially over many years – it can become a profound source of comfort. But of course, nothing can entirely prepare you for death – yours, or the death of those close to you.

If I didn't have my faith, I think I would be more reluctant to face my own mortality. For Christians, dying is about an end to the physical stage of life. For me it doesn't make sense that God, who has a loving purpose for us, should cut this off when we die. This is why I believe there is some kind of afterlife which follows on naturally after we die, in which God continues to care for us. Of course we don't know what the afterlife is like. This hasn't been given to us. But for me personally, the afterlife is a dynamic picture where we can continue to grow and develop – to become more and more alive.

Anyway, I hope so. Eternal rest sounds rather boring.

These days, people do have some pretty odd ideas about death and the afterlife. Some may be committed Christians but don't believe there is one. Others will say they do not believe in God, but believe in an afterlife. It's all about individual interpretation.

I think people are not so fearful of death itself, it's more to do with the fear of dying. It's normal not to want to let go of those we love. Nevertheless, faith can help us to find a way through our fear, so we don't collapse towards the end.

Most people these days do not have a classic deathbed experience, in which day by day and hour by hour a person can be seen to be leaving this world. I think that's a pity because this leave-taking can be very precious, as I experienced with my father.

At the time my father died, I was working as a parish priest. His death was an extraordinary process for me because he died during the Easter period. I lived 25 miles from him, so would go backwards and forwards from talking and preaching about death and the resurrection to sitting with him.

I particularly remember on Maundy Thursday staying in a darkened church after the service, symbolically keeping watch with Christ, and then getting into my car and driving to my father to do the same with him, but in a different way. The interactions of these two worlds became very powerful for me, especially when my father found it increasingly difficult to convey to me what he wanted. I found I was able to draw parallels between the silence of Christ at his trial and his gasped words the gospel tells us he uttered from the cross, and what was happening to my father.

The fact that I was interpreting one world into another made the process much easier for me. I think if our culture loses the Easter story – not just the vague knowledge of it, but the very details – we will be losing something that helps us to interpret our own life experience.

I haven't worked as a parish priest since 1992, and these days I do very little ministering to the dying. But I don't think you lose your instinct about the right time to do or to say a particular thing to the dying, or to their relatives. For instance, someone might want to be anointed or receive final communion. You can leave it too late, or it can be offered too early. You can't know, but you just feel it. It happened sufficiently often to me while I was a parish priest to think it was the work of the Holy Spirit guiding me. It also happened when a close colleague died recently. During his stay in hospital I went to see him several times, and just waited for the time to feel right before I administered the last rites. He died three hours later.

I think it's also important to recognize that a significant change takes place in the type of ministry you give someone who is terminally ill, as opposed to the time they are beginning to die. An ill person may want you to sit down and spend some quality time with them. But they may well reach a stage when it's not appropriate or possible to have conversations anymore. It's about recognizing when these conversations cease to be life-giving and become life-draining. Nonetheless, you keep appearing every day, perhaps for only five minutes at a time, but it's now about holding their hand and saying a prayer which helps them on their journey. The fact you are there, and they can rely on this, becomes very significant for them.

Unfortunately, these days many people find it difficult to know how to ask for help at the end of life. I've been a priest for more than 30 years, and I have never been called out in the middle of the night. People will call a doctor, but not a priest. I think guilt stops many from asking. Even though it is extremely rare for a priest to agree with this, relatives often imagine, 'Well, he or she hasn't been to church for years – none of us have – so we would be hypocritical if we ask the priest or vicar to come.' There is also considerable growth in secular funerals. But it's interesting to discover that many of these services include Christian teachings and psalms.

Another factor is the way in which communities have disintegrated. Many villages have become dormitories for those who work in large towns or cities – or second homes for those able to afford it. So our sense of security and belonging can cave in when we become ill, and there is no sense of cohesion to help.

I think the most important thing to do for someone who has a terminal illness is to help them to face the truth of what is happening, to enable them to be as honest as they possibly can – although I realize this is not always possible. Sometimes patients don't know what to say, nor do relatives. So everything is left unsaid. But I am sure if you come from a family where there has been honesty, the last thing you would want to do is turn it into some kind of deceit at the end.

Our hospital chaplains are very well trained these days. Their role is to support medical staff and, where possible, facilitate these conversations. Gentle questions can help people to know if they really want to pray rather than giving an answer they feel they ought to. They may say they don't want to pray, but will tell you how angry they are. That provides another opening for honesty.

I think it's the responsibility of all of us who work in the Christian ministry to talk openly about death and dying. We need to encourage people not to regard it as a taboo. For instance, when I preach, I always use the words 'death' and 'dying'. I would never talk about someone passing away, or falling asleep. When my time comes, I have already made it known that I want people to make a point of using the words 'He has died'.

You can't tell how you are going to die, but if I do have the opportunity to die gradually, I hope I will use the time creatively. I think when someone's death is well managed by medical staff and by relatives it can be rather wonderful.

It's important to talk about death, and to witness it, because it helps to lessen our fear. Often people who are open to this find spiritual and emotional fulfilment towards the end of their life. And I believe you want your last phase of life on earth to be positive – rather than your undoing.

The Muslim chaplain: testament of faith
Rehanah Sadiq

Belief in the afterlife is fundamental to the Muslim faith. It is one of the core articles of belief.

When a Muslim has a terminal diagnosis, it is not unusual for their family to take on the responsibility of breaking the news, rather than leaving it to the doctor. To lessen the shock, particularly for those who do not have a good level of English, or those who are elderly, the family will take into consideration whether the person is strong enough to cope with the news, and who should be present when they are told. For example, it may be better for a family member, even a close friend or a religious figure such as the Muslim chaplain, to tell them instead.

Some families may wish for their dying relative to learn about what is happening to them in a particular way – so information about their diagnosis is kept away from them until the family feel the time is right. This could be weeks or months, depending on the severity of illness. Other families will tell the person immediately.

However, and whenever, the news is broken it is essential for the dying person to be given enough time to prepare spiritually for their coming death. They do this as they begin to recite the Testament of Faith, 'La-ilaha-illalahu; Muhammad-ur-rasoolullah' which means, 'There is no god but Allah/God; Muhammad is the messenger of Allah/God.' This declaration is what makes a person a Muslim.

If the person is unable to make this recitation as the end of life nears, those around the bed will chant the Testament of Faith so the dying person can hear it and say it in their heart. Medical staff often struggle with this, because relatives and friends pack the room, coming and going all the time. But this is just part of our Muslim tradition.

Muslims are generally brought up in a culture which not only speaks openly about death, but encourages an awareness of how good actions in this world will lead to betterment in the afterlife. So it is quite normal for Muslim children to ask questions about death and dying.

I was 12 years old when I first saw a dead person. The body had been brought back home. It was customary (especially during the days of the first-generation immigrant Muslim community) to encourage children to take part in mourning rituals, and to help them understand that the soul of the dead person had gone to be with Allah, in a different dimension.

When my father died, I sat all the children down and explained in simple language how they would see their grandfather in his coffin, in order to allay any possible fears they had. I said that grandfather would look as if he was sleeping, although he would not be able to move because his soul was with Allah. Even though grandfather's body would physically decay, we were only saying goodbye to him temporarily. We will see him again when we eventually join him in the afterlife too.

Customs are beginning to change with second-generation and third-generation Muslims. For example, the body of the deceased is now normally viewed in the mosque rather than at home, and some younger parents wish to protect their children from seeing relatives and friends weeping beside the body. However, children cannot avoid the issue of death within the family. The Muslim community is strong in its ties and this makes all the difference. Everyone comes to the house of the bereaved family. It is a time to be together, to communicate with and support one another. There is an expectation for all relatives, extended family, neighbours, friends, and even those who may be complete strangers, to come and pay their respects.

This applies not only to the immediate family. My brother's father-in-law died recently. I was ill and unable to go to the funeral, but my children went, and so did everyone else. I knew then that I would have to make a special trip to pay my respects to the family, even though I would have to travel out of town. It is just expected.

From what I have seen, the Muslim culture in relation to dying is quite different from that in the West. For example, a beloved grandparent may go into hospital and the grandchild never see them again. The person dies and their body is kept in the mortuary until the funeral. The child may not go to the funeral and, even if they do, the coffin is usually closed. So they never have a chance to say goodbye, and they only learn about dying from the way their parents, or other adults, choose to describe it. Therefore they are disconnected without real experience or involvement. I find that terribly sad.

I have a lot of Christian friends with very similar beliefs to my own. They are happy to talk about the afterlife and going to a better place. But I also know people with no belief at all. They are not even agnostics. They believe that death is the end. My heart goes out to them. I cannot imagine what that must be like. I get so much solace and comfort from my faith when someone I know and love is dying.

Faith helps the grieving process too. I know of a Muslim woman who died recently, whose brother was unable to get to her in time. It caused him considerable grief and guilt. But we say to those who arrive after death has already taken place to remember the teachings of the Prophet Muhammad. One of the sayings from the *Hadith* talks about a man who has died, being able to hear the footsteps of those carrying him to the site of burial. He says to them, 'Take me quickly, take me quickly.' The dead man wants to go to the afterlife where he will be given the great fruits of the other world. So the brother was able to take comfort in knowing that his sister had gone to a better place. Muslims still feel they can speak to their deceased relatives, expressing their feelings and saying their goodbyes to them, believing that they are being heard.

In this Western culture, people are always taken care of physically when they go into a hospice, but their spiritual needs may not necessarily be met. Unfortunately there is no easy empirical way of measuring just how much pastoral care can help. But in my experience, the effect that spiritual care has on patients and their relatives is profoundly moving. They are so grateful because we can help their end-of-life experience to be dignified and meaningful. It makes all the difference.

Some time ago, I was called out to see a Christian woman. Her husband, who had converted to Islam, was dying. She wanted a female Muslim chaplain to help her understand what to do. While we were talking, I discovered she was a devout Christian. She desperately wanted to talk to someone with whom she could share her belief in the afterlife. I was able to do that with her, and empathize with her wholeheartedly. It was lovely to be able to support her and share so much that we had in common, even though we didn't come from the same faith background.

The Rabbi: a ritual path

Rabbi Lionel Blue

In Judaism, there is a lot of ritual around dying, which helps. Mourners create a family event, and we also have what is known as Holy Companionships. These are volunteers from the synagogue who offer to wash and lay out the body and make sure it's clothed properly, so the dead are not left in the hands of strangers. This feels much better for the family.

Speaking as a Rabbi, my personal attitude to dying is, of course, affected by a long tradition of Jewish attitudes and customs. Death is regarded as a ritual path, and the very act of dying washes away our sins.

Jews believe that when we die, we go into God's world, but that's not our business. It's God's. Personally I see it as trusting that the same force that brought me into life will see me out. What lies beyond is about trusting that this force, which made me, is not going to disappear on me.

Our business as Jews is about focusing on the living world until the moment of death. So the most important thing a Jewish man or woman can do is to make sure that the people who survive them are not left with an awful mess. This means writing a will and, as far as possible, making amends with broken relationships so the dying person can be at peace with their memories as they reach the end of life.

I remember how my grandparents, and many of their generation of Jews, would leave a small corner on the ceiling unplastered. It was there as a reminder that this life is not permanent. I agree with that. My intuition tells me that this is one stage of a much longer journey. What part of my ego survives death, I have no idea. But death is not the end of it. Therefore I can cope with life and what it throws at me in a better way.

I think you have to balance out knowing too much – or thinking you do – and knowing nothing. I think we decide when we are born and when we die. So dying is like waiting in an airport departure lounge. You have to make yourself as comfortable as possible, and then you are off.

Whatever religious or spiritual belief we may have, none of us know what is going to happen after death. Speaking as a Jew, I believe we possess a divine element, which is not subject to the laws of decay. So,

God's divine image is within us all. Nevertheless, to comprehend what life means after death is beyond space and time. It's impossible to know. Mortality is part of the condition of existence. It's part of the contract. Of course, death is much less tragic when you are elderly. The problem is when children and younger people die. I think the only way to make sense of it is to trust in the belief that death is not the end, but in the words of the Old Testament of Job, Chapter 1, 'The Lord has given and the Lord has taken away. Blessed is the name of the Lord.'

People don't talk enough about dying. We're all going to go through it. This isn't necessarily coming from a Jewish perspective, but you have to make peace with the fact that you are going to die; to know what you want; how far you may wish to prolong your life, or how far you want to go with pain control.

As a Rabbi, if people want to know they are dying, I discuss it with them. If they don't, I would never force it on them. Who knows anyway? I have heard of terminal patients who have been given the last rites and then they miraculously get well. I will admit that this is rare, but it has happened. Many people also ask me what happens when we die. But you can't prove what happens and you can't disprove it either. I think you just have to make the best of what is happening to you. In my own life, any problem I have I try to see it as God might, which can turn the problem inside out. I don't think dying is any different.

So, it's about embracing the knowledge that life does not last for ever. Mind you, I wouldn't want it to. Let's face it, life isn't built for happiness – and I think there comes a point when you will have had enough.

Personally, I don't have a great problem with death. Perhaps this is to do with my Jewish faith, or the fact I'm almost 80 years old. I'm not sure. But I am sure I don't like pain very much. Some people can cope with it. Others can't. I want to be able to control my own pain. That matters a lot to me and to my peace of mind. Being able to make choices about pain control takes the worry out of things.

Mind you, there's an advantage to old age. You are free of the rat race. You don't have to network anymore. I am also learning faster about spirituality, and what that means to me, than ever before. I am not tied to clouds of ego, and I am aware that the horizon has shifted. Yes, you forget more, and memories go, and you can't do the same things. But I increasingly see the good in people. If I am going to another dimension, I can take this with me.

So, I am not frightened of death. Actually, I think I will be rather relieved at the point when I have had enough. I don't think there is a need to endure needless suffering in the name of science.

The Buddhist: the importance of community
Padmadaka

There are several different Buddhist traditions which have developed over thousands of years. But I am very aware that some of those traditions and rituals don't work for the Western mind. The Western Buddhist Order, which was founded in the late 1960s, draws from these different traditions to make it meaningful and acceptable to us, especially when it comes to supporting the dying.

Traditional Buddhism emphasizes a belief in rebirth. People are reborn depending on how they have lived their previous life. But Westerners are not brought up in a culture which accepts this. So when I am helping to prepare a funeral ceremony for one of the community who has died, I take their personal beliefs into account. I would never say anything about them or about a Buddhist belief that they wouldn't have agreed with. Of course, if the person really did believe in rebirth we could include this in certain chants or mantras to help them on their way into their next life.

The main thing we do for anyone who is dying in the community is to help them find ways of resolving unfinished business they may have. It's about recognizing where disharmony lies – for example, past actions that are causing them regret, such as broken relationships. We would encourage the person to unburden himself or herself by writing letters, having those important conversations or perhaps donating money to charity – whatever is necessary to help the process of resolving the past.

For instance, not so long ago a member of our community was diagnosed with terminal cancer. He asked for certain community members to sit with him regularly throughout his illness, and especially during the last six months of his life. He wanted them to meditate and read Buddhist texts with him. By doing this, he was trying to put his life in order.

He also wanted to create a funeral service that expressed what he believed without alienating his friends or family, as several of them were Christian. It was a very personal journey for him.

When it's done in the right way, talking about dying can really enhance your experience of life. You become aware of how precious your life is, and you stop taking people for granted. Personally, I reflect on death every day. I deliberately bring it into my morning meditation practice. One way I do this is by focusing on my breath. It reminds me that each time I breathe in, it is this which is keeping me alive right now. But one day – and I have no idea when that will be – I will draw in my last.

Knowing this certainty helps me to stay in the moment, and to make the most of every day. It also helps me to be more detached about those things which it is so easy to become caught up in, or to hang on to.

But the truth is that everything that we have is impermanent. Nothing ever stays the same. So it's important to notice this – to look at older people and know that one day I too will be like that. This makes me feel humble.

It also helped me when my mother died. She went into hospital to have a routine operation, but got an infection and died three weeks later. It was the most awful shock, and quite devastating. There was nothing I could do but be physically present with her. I found this hard. Even though I have practised and taught Buddhism for many years, it's a very different matter when it's your own mother who is dying.

Facing her death challenged everything I thought I knew. But my meditation practice did help me to be emotionally and spiritually there for her when she died. I was able to encourage her to let go, and to be as reassuring and loving as I could be – especially during the times I thought I couldn't do it anymore.

I was also aware that I did not want to avoid the grief I was feeling. It was too important for me, and for her. I have no idea where she went after she died. Whether you are a Catholic like my mother, or a Buddhist like myself, we can't say for sure what happens when we die.

After my mother died I got a severe attack of shingles, which lasted a few months. I was so traumatized by her death, and sometimes it felt as though life had betrayed me. It forced me into a period of profound reflection, from which I knew I did not want to extract myself. During this time I reflected on the many Buddhist teachings about death and dying, more of which I agreed with. But when it came to something as difficult as dealing with my mother's death, I did not want to use anything ready-made to make things 'better' for me.

I knew the best thing for me to do – and the most natural – was to accept what I was feeling and allow myself to fall apart. That's what my body and emotions wanted to do. So I let it happen. But to be honest, I didn't really have a choice. I just had a deep knowing that it would have been dishonourable to her, and to myself, if I hadn't experienced the pain.

At the time I thought I would never be able to teach again, or say anything that mattered to anyone. But things have moved on – as things do – and I continue to be fully engaged with my work as a teacher of Buddhism, and with my Buddhist community.

The Hindu: karma and reincarnation
Vikram Patel

When someone dies in the Hindu community, everyone is involved to one extent or another. This also includes children, because we don't believe they need to be shielded from death. The mental state of mind of the dying person is very important – as this will influence the manner in which they will reincarnate. Therefore, many Hindus at the end will refuse medication that can cause them to lose consciousness, or to become confused. In the Hindu culture, pain at the end of our life is viewed as karmic, and should be experienced so it can be released before our next life.

So the way a dying person prepares for death is vital. This also includes the family. We will conduct rituals and pujas (acts of worship) – everything we can to help the person let go, and to let go ourselves. This can mean the dying person taking part in ritual fasting, which helps them to relinquish the physical world. Sometimes doctors in this country don't understand this, but it's our way. We know it's not the end.

I belong to a Hindu community in west London. We usually don't talk about dying – we just recognize and accept that one day it's going to happen. It's just a natural part of life.

There are many traditions within the Hindu religion, but when it comes to death and dying, we generally follow what's laid out in the Vedas. That's one of our most sacred texts. We believe there is one God. But God can be worshipped through thousands of different expressions, which is why we have so many gods and goddesses. In India, you find temples dedicated to these gods and goddesses everywhere. There are only around 30 Mandirs (temples) in the UK. But every Hindu home will have a shrine where they will do regular pujas in front of a picture or icon of a particular god or goddess, who is the family's favourite divinity. For example, this could be Vishnu – the supreme God; or Parvati – the Mother Goddess; or perhaps Ghanesh – the Lord of Success. There are many, many more – it just depends on who the family is drawn to.

So our whole life revolves around worship, either at home, or going regularly to the Mandir or to bigger celebrations and festivals at important times of the year, or through a pilgrimage to a sacred site where gods or goddesses are said to have appeared. This could involve travelling thousands of miles to a temple, or a mountain. And of course there's the Ganges. Our most sacred festival is Kumbh Mela which happens every 12 years. It takes place where the waters of the Ganges and Jumna meet. It is also our most sacred place in which to die. We believe that when our ashes are scattered on to Gangamai (Mother Ganges) we can be released from Samsara (the cycle of reincarnation) and reach the state of Moksha (enlightenment).

This is very important because of reincarnation. We believe we have a soul (or Atman) which is immortal. So, for me, when I die my soul will survive, and I will return to this life in another body. But what type of body depends on what I have done in my last life.

That's why it is important for us to live a good, honest life, no matter what caste we belong to, and to make sure our deities see this through our devotions. So yes, we take karma seriously. How I behave in this life will affect what happens to me next. Some Hindus believe that if they lived a bad life, they can come back as animals. I don't. But I do believe that I must accept the life I have been given, and do the best I can so my next life will be even better. It gives structure, purpose and order to my life. I like that. And I don't find it difficult, because I was brought up to do no harm. That's why I am a vegetarian.

When someone is very ill, we do try to stick to the hospital rules, but whenever possible the dying person comes home. If they can't come home, we will take our rituals to the hospital. This can be difficult if staff object.

When my aunty died – she died at home – the whole family was around her. My cousin, who was the chief mourner, led the rituals, pujas and chanting from sacred texts to help her to prepare for her death, and to focus on the greatness of Brahman – the absolute reality of all things.

The pandit (Hindu priest) also came to bless her and to perform rituals to help her release her final breath. One of these was to tie a thread to her wrist to bless her and to sprinkle sacred water from the Ganges over her.

We put her on the floor – this is a Hindu tradition. Lying on the floor helps the dying person to feel closer to mother earth. It also made it easier for my aunty to breathe and for her soul to leave. In India, putting a dying person on the floor stops their body bending when it stiffens. This makes it easier when we carry the body on the bamboo stretcher to the funeral pyre. But in the UK this isn't possible, so we would use a funeral car.

After my aunty died, we covered her with a sheet until she was washed and prepared by female relatives. When this was completed, we turned her head to the south and stayed with her body. It would be unthinkable to leave her alone. We continued to chant prayers and were joined by other family, friends and neighbours who came to pay their respects.

Normally we try to cremate the body within 24 hours. We cremate bodies because we believe the sanctification of fire releases the soul, so only the body is left to burn. Traditionally we would pour ghee (clarified butter) to intensify the heat of the funeral pyre. But naturally, we can't do that in crematoria, so we use it symbolically. But we conduct a number of rituals, including placing rice-balls beside the mouth of the dead person to make sure they have sustenance on their journey, as well as pujas which invoke the fire-god Kravyada. We light a fire in a clay pot and place it on the coffin alongside flowers and grains of white rice as it goes into the incinerator.

Afterwards we light a lamp and keep it burning at home for ten days, while the family withdraws into a time of mourning. During these ten days we do not eat meat, salt, or drink alcohol, nor do we wear perfume. We are expected to wash daily as a simple ritual, but not to cook. All our food is provided by neighbours and friends. And there is no entertainment – in fact, in many Hindu households, the family will not greet anyone or return a greeting.

After the tenth day, we conduct other rituals until the thirteenth day, which marks an end of the mourning, and the family return to normal life.

So, for me, my Hindu faith is about a profound spiritual preparation, and my own relationship with the different expressions of Brahma. This governs every moment of my life until it is time for me to draw my last breath in this particular body.

Up until now, this book has been focusing on the professional side of how death and dying are spoken about. An equally important consideration is stories from ordinary people who struggle in their everyday lives to know how to talk about the dying process, or who are forced into a collusion of silence when others refuse to engage with it. Therefore, the next chapter looks at the impact that a denial of death and dying has on personal relationships, offers guidance on how to broach this difficult topic, and explores ways to have *the* conversation.

CHAPTER 5

Having *the* Conversation

There are many reasons we avoid talking about death and dying. We may be embarrassed by our lack of knowledge, or we may be afraid of offending someone if we bring up the subject. Most of us have never got close enough to death and dying to have a relationship with it anyway. Consequently, we tend to live in a culture that has constructed a collusion of silence around it. Even in the medical profession, there is often a reticence to talk about death and dying as doctors attempt to change their focus from 'cure' to 'care'.

Linda, a counselling co-ordinator, believes that one of the main reasons why we find it difficult to talk about dying is a fear of getting it wrong and making the situation worse. 'As a culture', she says, 'we are not good at expressing ourselves. We are not good with people crying either. We don't want to see someone's suffering, and we do not know what to do.'

One interviewee said that perhaps we cannot bear to talk about death because life is such a struggle anyway. I think she may have a point. Another interviewee told me about a woman who has a brother with a brain tumour, her mother has dementia, her father has heart failure and not long to live, and she, herself, has just discovered a lump in her breast. So what *do* you say in this situation?

Tough though it may be, the answer is to just be there for them. It's about providing a safe haven for when they might want to talk, and to *listen* to them (for more information on good listening skills go to page 120). This means we have to come to terms with our own sense of helplessness and horror when hearing stories like this. But people are often very resilient. In the case above, the person is coping one day at a time by being very practical. Others might do things differently. So for those relatives, friends and carers providing support, it's about being sensitive to what each person needs.

Broaching the D-Word

Even though my father never regained full consciousness in hospital after his stroke, I was sure he could hear me. I knew he would have wanted to know what was happening to him, so I told him he was dying and that we were doing everything that we could to make him comfortable. I had a strong sense that this comforted him. However, if he had not been so open about death and dying, I know that I would have struggled to know what to say to him.

Others are not so fortunate, which is what Jenny experienced when visiting her friend in hospital.

> She was very lively still, and told me she was dying. I couldn't believe it and negated the whole situation. Later, when I saw her at home, she was in a coma and her breathing had become very laboured. I was shocked by her appearance and just stood there staring at her, when I should have sat with her, held her hand and talked to her. But her husband's grief was more than I could handle, so I left.

Jenny freely admits that she had no idea what to say or what to do, and this left her feeling impotent, embarrassed and guilty. But she also did not know where to find help or support so she could have handled the situation differently.

When relatives are in denial

I wanted to find out how other people experienced the fear of facing the death of someone they loved, and the effect that denial had on their relationship. The following four stories illustrate how each person coped in the moment. The chapter concludes with a summary of what can be learnt from these stories.

We start with Jane, a 42-year-old interior designer, who refused to accept her father was dying, even though, looking back, she realized he made several attempts to talk to her about it.

Although we were really close, I never spoke to my father about the fact he could be dying. It was too raw, too painful, to face the possibility. So when it happened, it was devastating.

I think my father tried to tell me on his 70th birthday. We went out for lunch, just the two of us. Afterwards, as we sat in the sunshine, having our coffee, he became a bit emotional. I thought, 'Oh God, what do I do here?' He mentioned that he didn't think he would see his 80th birthday – and that he would soon be seeing his parents again.

I felt totally helpless. I did not want to hear what he was implying. This was my father who had always been there for me. So I didn't respond. Anyway, it was his birthday. I didn't want it to become emotionally upsetting for either of us. I felt it just wasn't the right time.

Even when he was in the hospice, I still thought, 'No – it can't be that.' But I now realize that I was so disconnected from myself emotionally, I couldn't take it on board. I just couldn't bear the thought of never seeing him again. The result is that I live with regret and a sense of sadness I can't seem to shift.

Anne is a magistrate. Although her father was a doctor, she was brought up in a family environment where dying was never mentioned. This has had a long-lasting effect on her ability to cope with her father's death.

I was part of a middle-class family where emotions and thoughts were never spoken about. We certainly never mentioned death. I didn't know how to speak about it. It was too frightening. The trouble is that you then start to believe that if you eat properly and exercise, you will go on for ever. But it shuts out the inevitable and you end up brushing important issues like death under the carpet.

I was always close to my father, and was very shocked when he had a stroke in his late 50s. Although he recovered, I remember a friend saying to me, 'You are going to have to prepare yourself for him to die sooner rather than later.' But I had no idea how to do this. He eventually died of a burst aneurysm aged 78.

We were told by the doctors that he knew he was unlikely to recover. But when he called us to his bedside, neither my mother nor I wanted to go. I was so terrified, I remember pushing my mother in front of me to avoid being near him. But this meant I never took the opportunity to say goodbye to him.

I was devastated for months after his death. I know it would have been much easier if we had all been able to talk about it, but the thought of talking about dying still frightens me now.

James is an ex-advertising executive. He had a similar experience when his father was diagnosed with terminal cancer.

My mother wouldn't allow me to talk about my father's terminal illness either – he had Hodgkin's disease. She would say, 'Don't be so gloomy.'

The impact this had on me was one of confusion. A sense of keeping at arm's length not just the reality that my father was dying, but also my feelings about it.

At the time, I was living in Canada and about to get married. My wedding became a goal for him. He would send me letters with drawings of himself and a great lump coming out of his neck, accompanied by a row of exclamation marks, and the words, 'I will make it to your wedding.'

He arrived from the plane in a wheelchair – which was a real shock. He certainly knew he was dying and asked if I could 'do something' to help him to die. That was really hard because of course I couldn't.

When he returned to the UK he was taken off the plane on a stretcher. He died a month later. I still feel dreadful that I knew he was dying and I didn't come home to be with him. I certainly did not plan for how I would feel when he died either.

I can't blame my mother – her refusal to talk about my father was to do with the culture she was from. But it makes me sad to know that if only she had called me and said, 'Dad's dying, I know he would love to see you', I would have been on the next plane.

There was nothing wrong with his funeral as such. It's just that there was no respect or dignity to it. The vicar patted my mother's hand, but there was no acknowledgement of who my father really was. The truth is, my dad was a rascal. He loved his gin and played a squeeze-box, and told us rude stories about our relatives, the neighbours, and about the war.

My experience with my father has taught me that relatives need to talk to the person who is dying. And be available for them to talk too. That's just as important. I believe most people know when they are dying, so for their nearest and dearest to behave as if nothing is going on is excruciating.

Of course some people who are dying don't want to know the truth. It's their way of coping, and that's fine. But if you, as their relative, do want to say something, you have to have the courage to find a way of saying what's important for you.

Talking to interviewees, it became clear that a lack of honest and open communication within the family adds to the anguish of siblings. This was illustrated by Brigitte's story of how her family handled the death of her brother.

Brigitte now works as a health professional. When she was in her early teens, her 15-year-old brother was diagnosed with leukaemia. Although brother and sister were very close, during the eight months he was dying she never once spoke to him about it.

Two days before my brother died, I overheard a friend of my mother saying that you could tell when someone was going to die because their fingers turned black. I realized this was exactly what was happening to my brother, but I could not believe it. So I bought a bag of sweets for him, imagining that if I willed it hard enough, he wouldn't die. When I gave him the sweets, I knew there was no hope, but I could not bring myself to speak to him about it. I just pretended to be happy and cheerful. It was total denial.

To make things worse, my mother and father had the most spectacular fight over my brother's deathbed. My mum wanted him to die in peace. However, my father did not want my brother to die, so he ordered the doctors to use whatever means they had to save him. The doctors hauled in every machine they had and connected my brother to it. They pumped so much liquid into him that he blew up into a balloon. It made him vomit uncontrollably, and to this day my mother believes he literally drowned in his own fluids.

My mum went into such hysterics during the last hour of his life that the doctors had to call security. She was locked out of the ward, but she kept bashing mercilessly at the door, screaming for the doctors to let my brother die peacefully. After he died, my mother almost killed my father right there in the hospital. She was vile with anger towards him, and remained so for a very long time.

The impact this had on Brigitte changed everything in her life.

> I was a pretty good child before my brother died. But after he died, I became very irritable. I was no longer scared of what my parents could do to me. It radically affected my life because I started to cram everything I could into it. I got married very young and then travelled extensively with my husband. But I only really grieved for my brother ten years after he died. Then it took a very pitiful and tearful two years to finally accept his death.

What can help

- Admitting that someone you love is dying can be a source of great anguish. However, refusing to acknowledge that anything is wrong may be even more distressing to the dying person who, perhaps, might appreciate the opportunity to say goodbye.

- Some people are very open about the fact they are going to die. Although painful to hear, their willingness to engage can make talking about death and dying much easier for everyone.

- Having the courage to confront your grief means you can create special times with the dying person. These can become treasured memories for you both and can help the dying person find a sense of completion.

- Denial can cause family rifts between those who are willing to face the truth and those who are not. It is much easier for the dying person if everyone is willing to face what is happening. However, it is equally important to understand that for some relatives and friends this might not be possible.

- Be aware that unexpressed grief and anger, for example, over distressing childhood experiences, death of family members, or parental divorce, can surface years and even decades after the event, especially for siblings who might not, at the time, have received appropriate support.

- If you are struggling to come to terms with the truth of your relative's or friend's illness, or you are distressed by reactions and denial among those around you, do find someone to talk to who you can trust. It is a good idea if this person is not involved with the dying person or members of your family. This means they can be there for you, without emotional entanglement or expectation. Therefore, it may be better to talk to a professional counsellor. Ask your GP for recommendations.

- Acceptance can be particularly difficult when you have grown up in a family environment where dying is never mentioned. This can lead to a fear of talking honestly about it, or a refusal to accept the inevitability of death.

- GP surgeries often offer a free counselling service, or they will recommend local counselling services. This can be a very good source of help. More information on where to find help is covered in Chapter 7, page 101.

- It needs considerable courage to confront health professionals who talk in terms of treatment and cures, rather than about the actual person. Don't be afraid to challenge this or draw attention to the fact that this is, for example, your mother or father they are talking about. It's only by doing this we can bring about change in the way death and dying are spoken about.

- Take a look at the National Council for Palliative Care (NCPC) end-of-life strategy (http://www.ncpc.org.uk) or Help the Aged website (www.helptheaged.org.uk) for more information. Being informed helps you to deal with difficulties as they arise.

- Read through Chapter 8 of this book. It provides practical advice on end-of-life care.

When the dying person doesn't want to know

We have looked at what happens when relatives are in denial, but I also want to consider the distress that relatives and friends experience when someone refuses to face the fact that they are dying. Personal stories from four relatives explore what it was like to be forced into a collusion of silence, and how it has affected their lives.

The actress Sheila Hancock was forced into such a collusion when her husband, the television actor John Thaw, refused to admit he was dying.

In *The Two of Us,* Hancock's autobiographical account of her life
and marriage to Thaw, she wrote about his 'ability to box things
away'. Four days before he died, she found it particularly heart-
breaking to listen to him choosing the colour for his new Jaguar and
discussing whether he should sign up for another year with Carlton
Television. After a meeting with his specialist, who Sheila experienced as completely honest with them both, Thaw had turned to her
and said. 'Well, that all sounded very positive, didn't it, kid?' Later,
Sheila spoke to the doctor in private and urged him to make John
understand that he was dying. 'But the doctor told me, "I am sorry,
he just doesn't want to hear it and you have no right to make him
treat it any other way".'

Rebecca, a body therapist who is qualified to work with terminally ill patients, was distraught when her father refused to talk to
her about his illness.

He refused to admit he was dying, even when I tried to talk about the
practicalities of his illness. He completely closed up and told me there
was no point in having this kind of discussion. It wasn't going to
happen and he was in control of everything anyway.

But I could see he was dying. I had watched him disintegrate over
the past couple of years. I knew what I was seeing – I work with this
all the time. He lost a lot of weight and his face had gone grey. He
also found it increasingly difficult to breathe and suffered from
dreadful headaches. Sometimes he got so tired he would fall asleep
mid-conversation.

I felt angry with him for not being willing to talk to me. I was very
close to him, but found his persistent refusal to face the truth very
isolating and lonely. I feel as if I never really got to know the true
essence of him. That's left a big hole in my life.

But I do believe that part of loving someone is being able to be
there for them no matter what – even when it's excruciating and
awful. My father was eventually admitted to hospital after suffering a
major stroke. I watched him slowly disappear over a period of three
days. During this time, I gave him a lot of healing, held his hand and
gently stroked him. Even though he was unconscious, I wouldn't let
anyone talk about him dying while they were in his room. I was
passionate about that – you don't know how much a dying person
can hear. It's about being respectful.

His last few days were devastating for me but also, in a way, quite beautiful. When he finally died, the room filled with an incredible aroma. Both the staff and other family members commented on how wonderful this aroma was.

Rebecca was able to draw on her spiritual belief to help her through her father's illness. This helped her to find a sense of solace.

Although I am not a Christian as such, it comforts me to believe he has gone to a better place. Nevertheless, when someone dies whom you love very much, there's such a sense of final separation. So you need people around you to feel connection. Friends helped me a lot. But I found it hard to have to deal with my mother's grief on top of my own, especially as my parents had divorced many years ago.

Although Rebecca is still distressed by what happened, she says her father's death has helped in the way she works with terminally ill patients. But she still struggles to know how or when to bring up the subject of death and dying.

Should I take the lead? Or should I wait for them to open up the con-versation? In the many years of training I have done – including my qualification to work with cancer patients – death and dying were never mentioned once. It's such a sensitive matter that I believe a module for talking about death and dying should be obligatory for all those who train as therapists or work with the dying.

Belinda, manager of a personal coaching organization, found it equally difficult when her ex-husband and father of her two children refused to acknowledge he was dying.

We had been divorced for many years, but it was a strange relation-ship because I knew he was dying while his second family did not. I tried everything I could think of to help him open up – it didn't work. Even when he went into a hospice, he was in denial. There was never a conversation, so there was no opportunity to say goodbye. No opportunity to discuss his funeral arrangements or what he wanted. I found that terribly sad.

His denial also caused me problems with our son who was living abroad at the time. Although initially I never said in so many words, 'Your father is dying', I tried to alert my son to the seriousness of what was happening. But his father would email him, saying, 'I am doing really well. I'm fine.' At one point my son told me to stop talking about his father – I was making it worse than it was. But I made the decision to tell him outright that his father was dying so it wouldn't be a terrible shock when he came home. I didn't mention it again.

A couple of months later my son returned and was horrified to see how ill his father had become. I was so angry that his father had refused to talk about his illness. If he had accepted it, our son may have had the chance to have handled it differently.

It's really tough when people don't admit when they are dying. I believe my ex-husband's death could have been a far more healing experience than it was. He could have got a lot more support.

But it was good to see that, towards the end, he had become much calmer. It could have been the morphine, or the fact he was so near to death – I don't know. But, although nothing was said, it became easier for him. The pretence had gone. He stopped fighting and relaxed. He felt real, and so did the connection between us. It was also interesting to learn how much he wanted to reconcile with a few people from his past. I think these meetings helped a lot. I was so glad that he finally died surrounded by his children from both his marriages.

Belinda says her experience with her ex-husband has taught her a lot. 'If ever I am told I am going to die, I want it to be acknowledged and known and spoken about with those close to me. For their sake, just as much as mine.'

Amy, a 32-year old beautician, spoke candidly about the emotional effect that her sister's refusal to talk about her secondary cancer was having on the family, already grieving over the death of her brother a few months earlier.

We haven't had a final prognosis but it's not looking too good. It's difficult, as my sister doesn't like talking about it. She's also refused any further treatment. That's been very hard to accept from someone you love, and it's having a massive impact on the family. Surely you would want all the treatment you can have. But my sister just says the family doesn't know what she is going through, or what we are talking about. I can understand that, but how can we help her when she won't talk to us?

My sister's illness has been made worse because my brother died suddenly seven months ago of an undiagnosed heart condition. It was an unbelievable shock – so it's been an incredibly tough time. My grandmother died last year too, and my puppy almost died last week. So death is all around us.

Some days I am fine, but other days I find it very hard to handle what's happening. But I feel I have to be strong for my parents. They have enough on their plate. I don't want to appear upset because I don't want them to start worrying about me too. I feel I have to protect them – and my sister as well.

In an ideal world I would love to tell her how much I want her to stop racing around at a hundred miles an hour and to rest. To have counselling. To take on board the treatment she's had. But she doesn't want to know. We have all sat down with her in turn and tried to point out things that could help. We've also tried to encourage her to go to cancer support groups. But she won't engage. She's even torn up letters and cards sent by friends wishing her well.

I think she is terrified – especially after what happened to our brother. She doesn't want to die – who does? But I also think she is in denial – she believes she is the only person going through this. Talking could help her to realize that she's not alone, and she could find help with it all.

Personally, I feel very emotionally drained. I also worry all the time – that gets to you after a while. If I'm not worrying about my sister, or the dog, then I am worrying about my parents.

I think all this could be helped if we could start talking together – especially my sister. I just hope she will talk when she is ready. That's all you can hope and wait for – you can't force someone to talk or to have treatment if they don't want to.

What can help

- Of course you can't force someone to face the truth if they don't want to. This has to be respected. Denial is an important coping strategy for some people, especially if they are the type of person who has always swept important issues under the carpet.

- Some know they are dying and will speak about it. But they may not want to talk about how much time they have left.

- Even though this is difficult for you as a relative, friend or carer, it is not appropriate to expect people to change just because they have a terminal illness. People often approach their death with the same attitude as they have lived their life. Older generations, in particular, may have been brought up in a culture where stoicism was expected as a coping mechanism. It is not fair to expect them to behave any differently.

- Sometimes the dying – and their relatives – can find a cause to keep them going. This could be suing a hospital or medical staff for malpractice, or obsessively searching for cures, or perhaps prompting public awareness of their particular illness. Everyone has their own way of dealing with death and dying.

- However, colluding with someone else's agenda can be exhausting and exasperating. As a relative, friend or carer, you may well go through a complex mixture of emotions such as sadness, guilt and anger – even hatred and despair. Under the circumstances, these are not unusual reactions.

- Let the GP and hospital doctors know that you are willing to accept the truth of what's going on. They can provide you with support, especially when your dying relative or friend is nearing the end of life.

- It's worth bearing in mind that a dying person may be using denial as a way of protecting those they love. So make a point of letting them know that it's okay for you should they want to talk. Then leave it up to them if and when they want to respond. You could either write this in a card or a letter, or say it to them at an appropriate moment. For more information on broaching the D-Word, see Chapter 8, page 118.

- Be prepared for the dying person to change. They may want to talk the nearer they come to dying, or speak to a carer who they trust.

- Speaking *your* truth to someone willing to listen helps to lessen the burden. Ask your GP about local counselling services.

When there's no resolution

Family feuds can have a long tail on them. Siblings may have fallen out in childhood and never resolved their differences. Or there may have been physical, emotional or sexual abuse in the family. Children may have ended up in care. Others may have been abandoned at birth. One or both parents may have been addicted, for example, to drink, drugs or gambling. Or a parent may have suffered from a mental disorder, or simply have been emotionally cold. What's more, in the UK, some one in four marriages now end in divorce. It's not unusual for a parent to marry a number of times, or to have children with different partners.

All this can create complications and conflicts within families, which become particularly sensitive and volatile when parents start to die. Old resentments can surface and evolve into truly bitter battles.

Here are two very different personal stories about what it is like to face the death of a parent with whom it was difficult, if not impossible, to form a bond. We start with Keith, a 59-year-old writer, whose father died recently, aged 87.

My father was an emotionally distant man, so I never felt close to him. My parents divorced when I was 10, and my father re-married very quickly. Julia, my stepmother, dominated my father, which meant that he increasingly disappeared from my life. I hated her for that, especially when his whole attention became focused on her three children. It felt as if he had been stolen from myself and my siblings.

I reached a kind of truce with my stepmother after adulthood, but we always had a very superficial relationship. I never gave up, but it was hard to communicate with my father. Even our irregular telephone calls were always conducted with Julia in the background instructing him what to say.

But when he developed terminal cancer, I knew I wanted time with him – to see if we could at last have some kind of meaningful contact. By then he was in hospital, so I made several trips to see him over a period of a month. He was clearly dying. I tried to talk to him about it, but he gave me to understand that he just didn't want to know, or to talk about it. Finally I decided to tell him what I had always wanted him to know – how much I missed him as a father, and how hard it had been for us as children of divorce.

It wasn't at all an angry conversation, just a sad one. I think he understood, and there was a moment when he had tears in his eyes. But a minute later, when it was his moment to say something, he didn't respond to anything that I'd said, but asked if I knew when Julia would next be coming to see him.

A few days later, my father was sent home to die, still unwilling – or perhaps literally unable – to acknowledge what was happening. Our final telephone call ended with him saying to me, 'I just can't seem to shake this bug off.' How do you reply to that?

He died a week later, not having spoken about what was happening. But to my complete surprise, just the knowledge that he'd gone ripped the lid off a great box of suppressed rage about what happened all those decades ago. So, for various reasons, and as unexpectedly for me as for the others in my complex family, I realized that my place on the day of his funeral was not with my step-family and my siblings, but with my mother. Death hadn't provided that final reconciliation with my father, but we'd both gone as far as we could. So, at the moment of his cremation on the other side of the country, my mother and I joined in a quiet meditation in his memory, and then we went to the pub.

Joanna, a 53-year-old personal growth trainer, also faced intense distress when her father died. She had experienced years of sexual and physical abuse from him during her childhood, but wanted to find a way of reconciling with him. She quickly realized, however, that just because her father was dying did not change how he communicated with her, nor did it change the dysfunctional way in which her family related to each other.

When my father fell ill, I had no idea what to do. It was really awful to take my father's fragility on board, and to face the fact that the 'inevitable' was creeping nearer. As a family we never discussed the importance of money or wills. Consequently, I felt totally inadequate and invalidated when my father died.

This was made worse by the fact that my mother, sister and I continued with the unspoken dramas which had always peppered our 'normal' life. It got so bad that I used to go to see my father in the care home when I knew they wouldn't be there.

My father and I rarely spoke during my childhood and he could be very aggressive towards me. This didn't change while he was dying. In his last days he would roll over and turn his back on me while I sat for endless hours by his bed – wishing for the frozen silence to thaw. It did once – when he told me something he didn't want the rest of the family to know. So even while he was dying he expected me to continue the legacy of keeping quiet in order to 'protect' my mother and sister.

When the care home called me to tell me he was dying, I immediately jumped into my car to go to him. My mother, sister and brother-in-law were already there, but directly after he died they left the room.

I chose to stay with him. I closed his eyes, tidied his bedding and popped his slippers in their rightful place under his bed. Even though I knew he was dead, I was wishing for one magical unique last something to come from him. But it didn't. It was very hard to accept that there would be no more opportunities to connect with him.

When I finally left him, I found the night sister waiting in the corridor for me. I gave her a hug. It mattered to me that she was going to witness my father as a dead man. I wanted to shout, 'This is my father – and I only have one father! Please look after him – he has not always been a thin, yellow old man.'

Joanna has learned to make something positive out of her experience. 'I have taught myself to communicate with my father, now he is dead, in a very different way from when he was alive. Every night when I go to bed I tell him I love him. I have no idea if he can hear me, but the fact I say it helps me to soothe my soul.'

What can help

- If you have had a difficult or abusive relationship with your parent, very intense and conflicting emotions can surface for you when they begin to die.

- You may yearn for them to say something meaningful to you, or to ask for your forgiveness. This may never happen, so don't expect miracles. Your parent may be incapable of change, or unwilling to face what happened in the past you shared.

- You may feel such hurt and anger that you do not want anything to do with them, or to attend their funeral. You have to follow what is comfortable for you, even if that is difficult for other family members.

- Under these circumstances it's not unusual to feel glad that your parent has died. It can even be a liberating experience – as if a spell has been lifted. However, if you continue to struggle with feelings of anger, bitterness or resentment, don't let it fester. Although understandable, these feelings are toxic, and it's you who will pay the price – not your parent. So do ask your GP about finding a counsellor.

When children are not allowed to talk

During my interviews for this book, I was struck by the pain and sorrow that haunt those adults who, during their childhood, were actively discouraged from talking about a parent or sibling who had died. It prevented them from coming to terms with their grief, and that can make it hard for them to deal with death later in their lives, or to face their own mortality.

One story concerned a young man who had been killed in a terrible car crash while his father had been driving. The father survived and, shortly after the accident, came down to breakfast and announced to the rest of the family that 'This mourning period is now over. We are not going to talk about this anymore.' His son's death was never mentioned again. Twenty years later, during the opening minutes of a family therapy session, one of the siblings expressed such rage towards the father that the therapist had to stop the session.

Sally is 38 and works as a communication skills coach at board-room level. She is still impacted by the way her father's death was handled within the family.

My father died in 1980. I was 14 at the time. After he had been diag-nosed with terminal cancer, it was never spoken of again. As a family we had no support – or perhaps my parents didn't choose to seek it.

The first thing my school knew about his illness – he had been ill for six months by then – was my mother ringing to say that I wouldn't be in on 10 January as I would be attending my father's funeral.

After he died, I remember being on the phone to a friend. She asked me how my dad was. 'Oh,' I replied, 'he's died.' She became very upset. I felt it was my fault for causing her to cry, so I did my best to make it better again.

I had no idea how to tell anyone what had happened, and those times I did, no one knew how to react. I do not recall any of my teachers bringing it up or asking if I wanted to talk about it – or even saying something as simple as being sorry to hear about my father's illness, or the fact he had died.

After he died, he was never spoken of again. All his belongings were removed. It was as if he had never existed. That has stayed with me ever since.

Anna, a teacher now in her late fifties, burst into tears when she talked about what happened during the time her father was dying, and the consequences of not being able to talk about him.

My father died 48 years ago. I was ten at the time. He had been ill since I was born so I can only remember him as a disabled person. Somehow my siblings and I didn't know he was going to die. No one talked to us about it. I guess my mother thought it was clear he was getting worse and didn't think there was a need to explain. But as a child you don't put two and two together. I don't criticize my mum, she probably hadn't realized we didn't know.

I remember my mum waking us up to go to school as normal and telling us Dad had died during the night. We were completely shocked. The only thing I could think of to say was, 'Well don't worry, we can still have free school meals.' I said this because we were terri-bly poor and I knew that children without fathers at school were given free school meals. I thought it would make my mother feel better.

When we arrived at school, I remember thinking, 'Am I supposed to tell someone what's happened?' But I didn't know if it was allowed – so I kept it a secret. It was different in those days because there weren't the lines of communication that are available today. So the teachers wouldn't have known.

Straight after school, we were sent to stay with my two aunts for a few days. No one explained why we were there, or for how long. When we eventually returned home, it had been completely rearranged – as if my father had never lived there. It was the start of the conspiracy not to speak about him, and in all the years that followed, my mother and I only spoke about him once, right at the end of her life. I still don't know where he is buried and actually I don't know enough about my father to know how to talk about him.

I don't blame my mother, or the other adults in the family. We were so poor that her priority was to find ways of putting food on the table. I have a lot of time for this kind of stoicism – sometimes it is the only way to manage difficult things that happen. However, I am aware that it has made me very self-sufficient. I have developed a belief that to cope, I have to do it on my own. Maybe that makes it harder to trust others to do things for you – all the responsibility lies with you, and you alone.

These days, with an increasing awareness of the importance of allowing children to grieve, one would hope that Rebecca's story belongs to the past. Winston's Wish, a children's charity based in Cheltenham, has been a world leader in providing practical support and guidance to families, professionals and anyone concerned about a grieving child. They believe that the right support at the right time can enable young people to live with their grief and rebuild positive futures. This helps these youngsters to learn to deal with the life-and-death issues they will inevitably meet in adulthood.

Sadly, this is not necessarily always so. Another interviewee spoke about a very distressing story concerning two children of a friend.

Their parents lived abroad, so the girls were at boarding school in the UK. One afternoon, the father was tragically killed in an accident. Of course we were all devastated. But my first thoughts were for his daughters. So I set about finding out how to fly them both out to their mum as soon as possible. I was shocked when their mother said she didn't want them to come. She said she would fly back after the cremation.

This took place within three days of his death, so his body was never repatriated. Instead, the mother arrived back in the UK with his ashes. I found this particularly appalling because his mother was not given an opportunity to fly out to his funeral either.

The first time I realized that the girls were actively discouraged from speaking of their father was at a family celebration. I was talking to one of the daughters and mentioned in passing that her father had loved classical music. This was met by a stony silence from all those present, particularly her mother, as if to say, 'How can you bring up her father's name at an occasion like this?' It made me feel awful. So goodness knows how the daughter felt.

A year or so later, I had the two girls to stay – they were friends of my own daughter. I went out to do some shopping, and when I got back I found both sisters on their hands and knees studying photographs of their father from our photograph albums. Obviously they had asked my daughter to find the albums. They were desperate to talk about their father – it was like a raging thirst. They both wanted to know who had taken the photographs and who else was in the photographs with him. I was a bit taken aback at first, but then began to really, really enjoy talking to them about their father, and what I remembered of him. I could see the relief in their faces that it was okay to talk about him. I think this helped the two of them enormously.

What can help

- If you are unsure how to support a child who is facing the death of a close relative, or has been suddenly bereaved, do seek help. There is a list of helpful addresses and links on page 170. A particularly good website is Family Therapy UK (www.familytherapy.org.uk).

- Let teachers know what is going on. They will keep an eye out for how the child is getting on. Teachers can also suggest further support, for example, through the school's counselling system.

- Children need to make sense of death and dying. Usually with the support of a parent/carer or another significant adult, a child who has experienced bereavement can, over a period of time, learn how to process it and come to terms with it.

- Providing opportunities for the child to talk about intense feelings such as fear, sadness and anger, is instrumental in helping their long-term well-being.

- Being allowed to mourn is also essential for the child's psychological health. This means helping the child to take part in family rites and rituals around death and dying, which enable them to find some kind of acceptance.

- When a child is 'protected' from these rituals – such as stopping them from attending the funeral – the child can struggle to find a sense of closure or to recognize that the person has died. This often leads to emotional issues in adulthood, especially when faced with the loss of other close friends and family later in life.

CHAPTER 6

Sudden or Violent Death

Although this book does not focus on bereavement, many people find it particularly difficult to know how to talk to people who have experienced the sudden or violent death of someone close to them.

When a person is diagnosed with a terminal illness, they enter into a process which can give families and friends an opportunity to prepare for what is to come and to say their goodbyes. When people are confronted with sudden or violent death, their life is torn apart. 'There's no time to get your head around it,' said an interviewee for this book. 'Life suddenly became terribly insecure,' said another.

'I keep thinking, I wish I had done things differently,' said a third. 'My mother was knocked down by a motorcyclist and killed out-right. She had just popped out to the shops. Half an hour previously she had called me for a chat, but I was too busy to talk to her – I was really abrupt with her. I have to live with that for the rest of my life – and in my darkest moments, I wonder if it really was an accident or had I caused her to walk into the road without looking?'

'You never recover from it,' said a fourth. 'Even though it's five years since my sister was killed in a car accident, I still can't believe she will never come through the front door again.'

It can be very difficult to find a way forward when faced with traumatic experiences like this. The following interviews are stories from five people who speak about what helped – and what did not help – as they started to put their life together again after the sudden or violent death of someone they loved.

A brother's murder

Maria's brother, Gerald, and his best friend were murdered – both shot as they came out of Mass one Sunday evening during the troubles in Northern Ireland. She was 10 at the time; he was 18. It devastated the family, with the result that Maria retreated into a shell. She didn't talk about her brother or what happened for more than two years. But she remembers well her mother saying that people didn't know what to say to her, or wouldn't talk to her at all.

This prompted Maria's mother to set up a group for widows and mothers to come together so they could talk about what had happened to their husbands and sons. Most of them had never spoken about it either. Maria's mother went door to door inviting these women to come to the group. However, Maria continued to find it very difficult to talk about her brother, and that led to physical symptoms.

> Every time Gerald's name was mentioned, I would leave the room. It was easier not to talk about him and, through my parents' desire to protect me, we didn't discuss what had happened. Consequently, I bottled it up until I began to experience severe headaches, which led to suspected meningitis. I was taken into hospital and given tests, but the doctors couldn't find anything wrong.

What helped

> A doctor sat my parents down and asked them if there was anything wrong at home that could be causing me some kind of psychological distress. My mother exploded at the doctor, 'How dare you suggest there is anything wrong at home, when our son was murdered two years ago.' The doctor stopped her right there, and came straight back to talk to me about my brother. I immediately burst into tears, that's when I started to find some release from my grief and shock.

Maria's release of grief enabled her to embrace the belief that it seems as if 'things are meant to happen'. Her mother agrees with this.

My mother and I have often thought that if my brother had survived and his best friend had died, perhaps he would have been drawn into the troubles himself. And good has come out of his death. I have met some great people because of what happened to him.

It helps with my work as a doctor. I never say to the dying or to relatives, 'I know what you are feeling', because I don't and I can't. But if someone asks me if I have experienced the death of someone close, without going into details, I always say 'Yes'. I think this helps them to know I understand what it's like to deal with death and dying.

It has been 34 years since Maria's brother was killed, but, like others who have had similar experiences, she says she will never get over it.

There's still this emotional ache whenever I reach an important landmark. For instance, when I went to university, or graduated, or started work, or married – I was aware he would never get to do this. It still makes me feel angry and sad.

A car crash

Robin is a publisher. He was travelling back in the car to London with his wife and youngest son. A young man in a Volvo failed to realize that the road was not a dual carriageway. He drove into them at 70 miles an hour. Robin's wife was killed instantly and his son died in hospital shortly afterwards. Robin was hospitalized for several weeks.

The novelist William Trevor says, when a wife dies you are cut off from the past, but when a child dies, something of the future is blocked. The loss of my wife is terrible, but the loss of my son is worst of all. It will always affect me. He was so naughty and so cheerful and such a rebel and so cheeky – I was always chasing him round the dining-room table, but never able to catch him.

Robin believes nature has its way of helping people to survive. Visitors who came to the hospital to see him were amazed at how cheerful he was at the time. Looking back, he now realizes this was a symptom of shock, allowing him to survive what he came later to realize was terrible anger and rage. He didn't know it was there, so he couldn't express it. Instead, Robin forced himself to focus on bringing up his two other children. But he also became obsessed with the compensation claim. It wasn't about the money. It was about finding a way to cope with what had happened.

It took five years to get to the High Court to agree on a settlement. Afterwards, Robin remembers walking out of the building into Fleet Street and feeling completely alone.

It was all over – everyone had gone home, and I experienced this dreadful sinking feeling, which tipped me into a deep depression.

A couple of months later, I was taken to Mexico by my cousin. I can remember one morning waking up and physically convulsing with rage. It was the most extraordinary experience, but once it had passed, I felt my depression lift and I was able to start engaging with life again.

What helped

At times, it was acts of kindness from friends and relatives. My two children came to the hospital immediately – they wanted to make sure I was alive, and so did my wife's family. I also received hundreds of letters and flowers.

My brother, with whom I had had a complicated relationship, dropped everything to be with me. I was very touched by that. And the best people were those like a friend who arrived by my bedside and said, 'Right tell me what happened'. That was fantastic. A hospital priest was also very good. Rather than pretending to know what to say, he just said, 'Robin, I don't know what to say'. I really liked that. But you also need practical help, such as someone to fill your deep freeze with food, to offer to hang out the washing, or mow the bloody lawn and take your daughter to her party.

Both my children had school counsellors, which helped too. About a month after the accident, one of counsellors rang me to say, 'I think you should know that your daughter doesn't actually know what happened. I think you should tell her.' That had never occurred to me. I had taken it for granted that both children knew. So I sat down with them and told them the events of the day in detail – all the way through. It helped all three of us to know it hadn't been my fault.

On the tenth anniversary of my wife's and son's death, I organized a memorial Mass. Both my children did a reading. But the really nice thing was the number of my deceased son's friends who came – some with girlfriends and jobs, others looking crazy. This was how he would have been had he lived. Seeing this did my elder son a lot of good. I think he felt a sense of community with his brother again. It was also very therapeutic for me.

What did not help

A nurse who said to me, 'You should turn your mind to the Man upstairs'. That really got to me. Although I am a practising Catholic, I wanted to murder those who thrust religious books at me.

Quite soon after I had started to recover from my injuries, I became the object of female interest, some of which I found quite amusing to deal with. So even tragedy has its funny side.

I also remember being at a party when someone I knew well caught my eye and then walked out of the room because he didn't know what to say to me. It's understandable, but I found it sad he couldn't even say 'I'm sorry.'

A positive thing Robin says he has taken from this whole experience is the importance of being reconciled with his children on the few occasions they have had bust-ups. Another is that he still considers himself to be part of a unit of five people. He concluded, 'I know that two of them are in heaven. This wipes away my fear of dying.'

A sudden heart attack

Gwen also found that small acts of kindness helped her to make progress after her husband dropped dead in front of her. He had suffered from heart problems for a long time, but had been doing so well that he had been discharged by doctors.

> One morning he brought me a cup of coffee, got back into bed beside me and died. Just like that. I didn't have a telephone in the room, so I screamed out of the window for help. Luckily my neighbour was in her garden and heard me. She immediately telephoned her daughter who was a nurse. She dropped everything to come and help. In the meantime I called 999. The person who answered just stayed with me on the line and then told me exactly what to do and how to try and revive him. But of course I couldn't.
>
> Paramedics were fantastic when they arrived. They worked on him for quite a while before taking him to hospital. The GP arrived too. She knew exactly what to do, and made it quite clear that a post-mortem would not be necessary. I was very grateful for that.

Over the years, Gwen's husband had undergone a couple of major heart operations. Even so, they never talked about what might happen in any great depth. Nor had there been a conversation with his doctors about the possibility of him dying.

> But I knew what the situation was. That's why I insisted on him giving up sailing, which he loved. I told him it was because I was fed up with feeling sea-sick. But really I had had enough of being terrified of finding myself mid-ocean and wondering what to do if his heart gave out, leaving me to cope not just with him but also the boat. So in a way I was prepared, but you never really are. It's such a terrible shock when something like this happens.

What helped

I suppose one of the things that helped was knowing that my husband wouldn't have wanted to be in hospital or in a care home. Family and friends were also fantastic. So was a neighbour who turned up after the ambulance left and just sat with me. He didn't say very much, but he didn't need to. He only left when my family arrived.

As soon as I told my daughter-in-law, who is Greek, she went straight to the shops and bought traditional Greek ingredients for a meal 'for all eventualities'. It included chicken, rice and potatoes which could be cooked on top of the stove. It was such a comfort to know that something as normal as cooking was going on in the background of such emotional chaos. Different people were pitching in to help as well. I think you are in such shock that it becomes 'the more the merrier'.

I also found it very helpful when my daughter-in-law's mother said traditional Greek ritual mourning prayers for my husband on particular days. It was lovely to know she was doing that, even though she lived in the USA.

It made me realize the importance of mourning. People don't know what to do or how to behave these days. So yes, ceremonies and traditions matter. But I did receive a huge amount of correspondence and cards. I found that very consoling – and the fact that neighbours kept dropping by to see how I was.

Before the funeral, I went to stay in London with my son and daughter-in-law. She took me out to all these designer shops to buy a dress for the funeral. When I got back home, another friend took me shopping for accessories. I know this sounds dreadful, but I found keeping busy – even if it was shopping with a friend – really helped me.

Gwen said that being part of a small village community has been very supportive and nurturing, particularly as she met her husband while they were at school together.

So I had never known life without him. He was the outward-going one, and I was the one who tagged along behind. But, after he died, I was able to slip into doing more things in the village – and I also went away quite a bit. So I have found that it's about doing things that helps, rather than moping about.

Most people were really good about it – they didn't shy away, and some weren't too sure what to say. But there's nothing much anyone can say, except how sorry they are. I would prefer that to them walking away.

It's been almost two years since Gwen's husband died. It comforts her to know that other people are still grieving for him.

I like it when they talk about him, or give a sardonic comment about him not approving of this or that. I also think sobbing is good – I just wish that, as a culture, we did more of it.

A miscarriage

During her late teens Chris was diagnosed with cancer. After surgery and chemotherapy Chris recovered. Although she was told it was highly unlikely she would ever conceive, she married and had a son. Six years later, to her surprise, she found she was expecting another baby.

Because of my medical history, when I discovered I was pregnant it was as if a dream had come true. I desperately wanted a girl and was overjoyed when the scan confirmed that I was to have a daughter, who we named Lydia. I could feel her moving but, at 20 weeks, I began to experience blood spotting. It didn't stop so I was admitted into hospital to have another scan.

I will never forget the doctor saying to me and my husband, while having the scan, that they were sorry, but they couldn't find the foetal heartbeat. At first I couldn't understand what they were talking about. Then they told us that the baby wasn't alive anymore.

I was then told I would probably have to be given some medicine to 'get rid of the foetus'. That really hurt me. This was my baby they were taking about.

I was bleeding quite heavily by the time I was taken to the ward to be prepared for an operation to remove what was in my womb. Just before the operation, I went to the toilet and passed what I realized was my baby. It was awful to know that the daughter I had loved so much and hoped for had ended up in a toilet bowl.

The day after the operation I went home, and had to tell my son what had happened to his baby sister. He was devastated. But I found it really hard to be with him. He wasn't the baby I had lost. That made me feel terrible.

It was also hard because I had nothing tangible to grieve over – there was no body to bury. All I had were the memories of her being inside me. My husband was very supportive, but he seemed to get over it much quicker than me. But he didn't know Lydia like I did. He hadn't carried her in his body like I had. And every morning I woke up feeling this aching empty hole, and unable to come to terms with it.

What helped

A friend said it was important to say goodbye properly. So a week after the miscarriage, we held a little service of remembrance for her. We said some prayers and read poems, and listened to a few pieces of music. It was my way of acknowledging she had been a life to me.

I also made a memory box for her. We put into it what would have been her new cot sheet, some pressed flowers, a pink candle and the Order of Remembrance service. I kept her box for years, and have only recently buried it under the tree we planted in the garden to mark the day she would have been born. The tree is quite big now, and has the most wonderful blossom every spring.

Other women had been through the same thing and had gone on to have other children. Their stories gave me hope. In fact, within a year of this happening, I gave birth to my daughter, who is now 11.

A woman who was in her seventies wrote a wonderful letter to me telling me that she had experienced a miscarriage at the same age as me. She had gone on to have other children, who had also had children. But she had never forgotten the baby she miscarried. It made me realize I was a part of a group of women of all ages who had once gone through the same as me, and it was normal to feel grief.

The consultant was very kind. He told me that when it's a healthy pregnancy, there is nothing you can do to lose the baby. But if the pregnancy is not healthy, there is nothing you can do to keep the baby either. His words helped me to release the guilt of believing I had caused the miscarriage because I had done something 'wrong'.

What didn't help

People who told me I could always try again. Or, at least I had a son and wasn't I lucky. There was no acknowledgement of what I had gone through or that I had lost my daughter. I didn't want to try again. I just wanted Lydia back. I found these comments, however well-meaning, cruel and insensitive.

Friends who sent bouquets of pink flowers. I kept on thinking I should have got these when Lydia was born, not because she had died. The best bunch of flowers I received was from a friend who had also experienced a miscarriage. She brought me bright yellow tulips which reminded me of springtime and life.

A week or so after the miscarriage I found myself back in hospital. A doctor who was pregnant herself came to see me. Her manner was very brusque, and she asked me how long ago I had had the 'termination'. I was so upset I couldn't say anything. My friend who was with me was so incensed that she made an official complaint against the doctor.

I was brought up as a Catholic. I found it very difficult to accept the concept that if a baby is not baptized it has no final resting place. The thought haunted me for a long time. It also meant that my parents found it difficult to acknowledge her existence. They thought I was grieving unnecessarily.

I don't consciously think of Lydia so much these days. My daughter's growing up has taken over. But I never forget her because every day I look out of the window and see her tree. So it's not painful anymore – more like a bittersweet memory. And I am very aware of the gift she left me, which is to really appreciate the son and daughter that I have.

Providing appropriate support

- It's normal to feel awkward or embarrassed when meeting someone who has been suddenly bereaved, especially for the first time after the event. Even if you don't know what to say, rather than crossing the street or walking out of the room, make a point of saying something as simple as, 'I'm sorry to hear what has happened.' Then leave it to them to decide if they want to talk about it. Or you could write a card.

- It's also important to know that nothing can make the situation better. Like the priest who visited Robin after his car crash, it's about being there to listen when needed. And being willing – and able – to cope with someone who is either completely traumatized, numb or in extreme shock.

- This may make you feel helpless around this person – a perfectly usual reaction when we are unable to 'do' anything to fix things. If you can learn to sit with your discomfort, you will be the support that this person needs.

- Don't pretend you can possibly know what the person is feeling or experiencing. Or indeed ever will. You can't. That's why no one can judge how a person is coping. Everyone deals with trauma in his or her own way and time.

- Don't tell the person what to think or what to do, or offer your own spiritual or religious beliefs. This can make the situation worse, especially when someone's life has been thrown into turmoil. Instead, *do* something practical to help, such as filling the freezer with food, or leave casseroles on the kitchen table, or take children to school. But don't take offence if your offer of help is refused. Just be on hand to help out when asked.

- It is not unusual for women to make themselves available to men who are suddenly bereaved. Do be sensitive around this. Of course men need support – so do women – but not necessarily the emotional complexity of romantic involvement at such a vulnerable time.

- Be sensitive to the fact that this person's life will never ever be the same again. Nor will they 'get over' it. But they may, in time, find ways to cope with what has happened. This can take years, if not the rest of their life.

- Don't be embarrassed to mention or talk about someone who has died. If you are not sure, ask the bereaved person if it's okay. They will often be delighted.

- Finally, be aware that hearing of sudden or violent death can throw up traumatic emotions in all of us. If this has been triggered in you, and you are finding it difficult to cope, do consider finding help.

Coping with suicide

When a person commits suicide, the shock of their action can feel like the force of a tsunami. It often leaves even those on the periphery of the person's life shocked, shaken and helpless to know what to do.

Suicide carries a stigma, because it is hard to take on board the extent of despair and hopelessness that could make someone kill himself or herself. Also, there is always police involvement and a coroner's inquest (often reported by local media) into the cause of death, so it becomes a public story. And perhaps because many friends and relatives, even neighbours and acquaintances, can feel outraged at such a 'selfish' act, or find that their religious or spiritual beliefs have been affronted, or perhaps they feel guilty for not 'having done enough', 'spotted the signs', or said something that could have stopped it.

So knowing what to say to someone whose relative or friend has committed suicide can be very challenging.

Fiona, Samuel's ex-wife, had attempted suicide once before. Then, one weekend when she knew no one could stop her, she killed herself with a drug overdose. Samuel found her on the Sunday evening, when he was dropping something off at her house. She had left a note on the stairs for him, asking him not to come into the bedroom, and to call the police.

At the time, I was pretty open with people about the suicide itself – what happened, the puzzlement of the coroner, the invasiveness of the emergency services. But I was selective with whom I told about her previous attempt.

I had been on the receiving end of quite a lot of blame after our separation and I was worried this would go to a new level after her suicide. But in fact, I think it helped people to understand the situation and the pressure I had been under.

Fiona had suffered from long-term depression. It was well known by her family and close friends. Some people were angry with her – that she'd 'wasted her life', 'been stupid'. But most were either very sad, or understanding that she had released herself from a life she found unbearable.

What helped

Samuel was deeply touched by reactions from close friends who, on hearing the news, immediately came to his aid.

They showed me love and understanding rather than blaming me, as they could have done. Fiona's family were also very supportive throughout the whole thing.

But I found therapy particularly helpful. Although Fiona made it clear in her note that it wasn't my fault that she had killed herself, I spent a lot of time working on my feelings of guilt and responsibility.

I also found piecing together her last few days helpful. She had visited friends for the weekend, seen a friend for lunch on the day she died, and was supposed to be at a party that evening. I needed to do this to try and make sense of it all.

What did not help

I remember being shocked when I overheard a friend who came round to be with me that night tell the paramedics Fiona had 'topped herself'. That felt disrespectful. 'Taken her life', or 'killed herself' is fine. But not euphemisms like 'topped herself'.

After she made her first attempt, she was admitted into hospital. I found it very difficult to see the way she was being treated like a naughty child by the staff. We ran out of the hospital before the consultant came. She wasn't having any of that.

But it's difficult to know that some aspects of what happened will never be resolved, such as no chance for one last talk, or to tell her that I still loved her. Or to come to terms with my thoughts about the level of pain and loneliness she must have felt. It's being left with the 'If onlys'. These went round and round in my head.

Even though ten years have now passed, Samuel still feels wary of people being interested in Fiona's suicide for the wrong reasons. He made the mistake of once mentioning it to a journalist. The journalist had immediately homed in on it as an interesting story, but did respect Samuel when he refused to talk about it. Samuel is still cautious of being judged or misunderstood. However, the main issue for Samuel is being left with the sadness that someone who wanted to die, who was really resolved to do this, had to do it alone.

When I think of it, I think of the risks involved of her not getting it right – the loneliness of it all. I would like to feel, if I was totally convinced by her that this was her final decision, that I would have been able to be with her. To comfort her and hold her hand.

Help and support

If you need further support on any aspect of suicide, Survivors of Bereavement by Suicide (previously know as SOBS) is an excellent resource (www.uk-sobs.org.uk). Alison Wertheimer's book, *A Special Scar: The Experiences of People Bereaved by Suicide* is also an excellent resource.

CHAPTER 7

Finding Support

Professional help

Some GP surgeries have a free counselling service, although the number of sessions is usually limited. Ask your GP for information, or about local counselling services in the area. Local counselling services often have charitable status and offer a 'Pay what you can afford' policy.

Many companies run an EAP service (Employee Assistance Programme) for their employees which entitles them to a set number of free counselling sessions. Ask your manager or Human Resources department for information.

To find registered psychotherapists and counsellors, look on the BACP (British Association for Counselling and Psychotherapy) website for those in your area (www.bacp.co.uk), or the UKCP (United Kingdom Council for Psychotherapy website, www.psychotherapy.org.uk). Their costs will vary and many therapists have their own websites explaining how they work and what to expect from therapy.

Although some people are more comfortable talking to friends and family about their issues, many of the people interviewed for this book found that talking about death and dying to someone experienced in listening skills was very helpful. One example of this was given by a funeral director.

Not so long ago, an elderly lady came to see me about her funeral arrangements. She told me she had had enough and she wanted to die. So I encouraged her to tell me about her life, which she proceeded to do at great length.

She also told me that after her husband had died, she kept his ashes on a sideboard in the kitchen. Every day she would take out one spoonful of his ashes and hurl them into the bin saying, 'And that's just where you belong.' I have no idea what her husband had done to deserve this. She never said, but the fact she told me was obviously liberating for her.

Soon after her visit, she bought a new car, went to New York, Barbados and Israel, and started speaking on the Women's Institute circuit about how great it was to talk about funeral arrangements in advance. Last heard of, she was working as a television extra. By the way, she is 83.

For Brigitte, whose brother died of leukaemia (see page 71), the listening skills of a counsellor provided her with a life-line.

It was only when I went into therapy that I began to understand that both my parents wanted the best for my brother. I could see how my mother had accepted that my brother was dying and had given him permission to die peacefully. I could also empathize with how my father refused to accept this and did everything he could – however futile – to save my brother's life. Being able to make sense of this released my own pain. I don't hurt anymore and have made peace with both my parents – who, amazingly, are still together.

Nick also found counselling invaluable after his wife was diagnosed with terminal cancer. He is in his mid-forties and works with businesses to improve corporate responsibility.

We had just moved out to the Far East. The doctor who broke the news to my wife told her two stories. One was about a 72-year-old Buddhist monk who had extensive cancer. The monk took it in his stride, and eventually died at the age of 84 of something quite unrelated. The second story concerned an American businessman, also diagnosed with terminal illness. He completely panicked and died within a short time. My wife immediately realized it was up to her how she was going to handle her illness, so we moved straight back to the UK.

From that moment on, she completely took control of what happened to her. In fact, I would say that her illness brought out the very best in her. She decided what treatments she was going to have, and what worked for her and what didn't. She also refused to wear a wig and used to go out with painted transfer tattoos on her head. She looked so radiant that lots of people thought she had purposefully shaved her head because of some kind of religious belief.

We made a conscious decision to be very open about what was happening to her, including with our two children. She was very keen for the children and myself to go to counselling. The kids didn't really want to, but it was incredibly important to me. It was a place where I could say anything I needed to someone who I knew understood what I was talking about – and I didn't have to spare his feelings either. This really helped me to make sense of what was going on for me.

The counsellor also normalized things for me, which made a huge difference. For example, he told me what I could expect as my wife's health deteriorated. Even though it was a truly dreadful time, just knowing what might happen helped massively.

I was able to understand, and be okay knowing that I started my grieving process some weeks before my wife died. By the time she died, I felt as if I had worked through a lot of it.

Saying goodbye was an incredibly important part of all this. The hardest thing was telling the children. She did this one afternoon while I was at work. I respected that she needed to do this in her own time and in her own way. It was her journey.

I took care of her until the last few days when her needs became more than I was able to provide. Even though her carers were fantastic, I found it very hard to hand over to them. This was our journey together, and now others were involved.

We had one final moment of connection, which was very precious. The first time she couldn't get out of bed was the day she died. By mid-day she was unconscious. Later in the afternoon I held her, and cried and talked to her. All of a sudden there was a movement, and her arm fell across me. That was the last movement she made, and I will never forget it.

She died later that evening while I was out with the children. Her

104   THE D-WORD

mother and a carer were there at the time. That bothered me for a while – I would have liked to have been there. But I now realize it was what she wanted. Anyway, she did seem to have hung on until my daughter got her exams.

My counsellor also explained about the post-grieving process – and how sometimes women make themselves very available after your partner has died. Exactly this situation happened, but I was prepared for it, so I didn't feel confused about the emotions I was having.

Overall, my counsellor helped me to get my life back. I will always remember him saying to me, 'Nick, you have a right to happiness.' I have now married again, and it's great to see how well my new spouse gets on, particularly with my daughter. She gives my daughter things that her mum couldn't, but I think my son still struggles with all this.

I think the way we talk about dying in our society is contextual. I had a better deal than some because my wife set the tone. Her approach liberated those around her. Of course there were those who trod on eggshells, but I refused to allow this. People will skirt around death if you let them. But if you are comfortable with it, you can help them to work out what they want to say. And those who don't want to just stay out of your way.

Mind you, I also believe I was helped by the fact I have lived and worked abroad. I am not saying I would want to swap my life but, especially in third-world countries, there is this sense of a spiritual connectedness to life and to death, which we have lost in our society. I think that's sad.

Paul, who is an occupational psychologist and bereavement counsellor, believes that most of us are emotionally unprepared to care for someone who is dying, or indeed to know how to express our grief.

The problem is that death has been moved out of the home. In the old days the family took care of the body; it was a normal part of life. But today, we pass it all on to the professionals to take care of it for us.

It also means we have no rules of mourning anymore, so no one knows what to do, or what to say. But we need to be able to make sense of life in order to come to terms with it. To make sense of life we need to be able to engage with what is happening around us. This means talking about difficult things like dying, or at least thinking about it.

Obviously this can be very hard because the truth is that people aren't very beautiful when they die, and it's human nature to skirt over unpleasant truths like this. But the danger is that when we don't talk about our distress, it can grow out of proportion and become unnecessarily frightening. For instance, I see many clients who come to counselling because of a recent bereavement. However, it quickly transpires that what is really troubling them is an earlier experience of someone dying that they have never addressed.

Of course not everyone wants to talk about death, dying or bereavement. That has to be respected. But I think it's about learning to be sensitive and, rather than cross the street to avoid it, it's about learning to calmly acknowledge the person with something simple like, 'I am sorry to hear you are ill, or that so-and-so has died.' People like that. It doesn't have to go any further either, unless the person wants it to.

Normalizing things also helps. For instance, I see many older people who are worried about talking out loud to their dead husband or wife – or seeing ghostly images at the end of the bed. They are concerned they are going mad and often feel they can't share this with other family members. So it's about listening to them without judgement, and allowing them to have their experiences.

Not everything is as clear-cut as this. Finding ways to support clients who have experienced a sudden death can be very challenging. Many questions remain unanswered and can leave relatives with feelings of incredible anger or guilt. Providing support is all about listening and allowing the person to find ways of coming to terms with what has happened.

Melissa, a psychotherapist who works in London, also believes that talking helps us to make sense of what is happening when someone dies.

Finding someone who is skilled in listening is very helpful because they are able to recognize inconsistencies, and gently challenge the person to confront what is really bothering them. This can be a huge release, especially when the person has been caught up in denial. To grow as human beings, we need to learn how to face the un-faceable. Many people have no inner frame of reference for how to deal with distress-ing situations. Counselling provides a safe containment in which to explore these issues and make some kind of sense of them.

The reason why people turn to counsellors is because we no longer have the sense of community that we did in the old days. We don't know each other anymore, but this means that we are very limited in whom we can trust when we are feeling vulnerable.

We find help when we feel seen and heard by someone who cares, but who is not emotionally invested in what we are going through. That's why it often doesn't help to talk to close friends or relatives. It's hard for them not to give advice or to talk from their own perspective.

Finding someone – whether that is a professional counsellor or someone you can really trust to be there for you – provides much-needed connection, particularly when facing something as emotion-ally fragmenting and volatile as someone close to you dying.

We all live with death anxiety. As we get older I believe we need to think about what that means to us, but not in a negative sense. Rather than focusing on how long I have got, it makes me intensely grateful for what I have. I treasure this.

How to support yourself

- When a close relative or friend is dying, don't be afraid to find someone to talk to early on – either a professional counsellor or a friend or colleague you can trust. Talking and being lis-tened to can lessen feelings of loneliness and isolation. This may be the only person with whom you can share the reality of the situation.

- Talking normalizes feelings. It also helps to structure your thoughts, so you can begin to make sense of what you are going through.

- Talking can also help you to work through difficult decisions that you will have to face after the person has died, such as caring for children, sorting out financial issues and the prospect of meeting a new partner when you are ready.

• Finding support enables you to work out the best way of helping children who will be experiencing loss in their own way.
You may need extra professional help and support when, for
example, you decide to tell a child that a sibling or parent is
dying or has been killed.

Speaking euphemistically . . .

Many of us use black or droll humour to talk about dying. Ask any
nurse, doctor or undertaker and they will say it comes with the job.
But this is not from a lack of respect or empathy. Humour helps to
defuse emotional intensity, especially when working closely with
those who are dying. We also use euphemisms to soften the blow,
and even to describe the dying experience with a sense of warmth
and affection.

   For example, 'Kicked the bucket', 'Fallen of his perch', 'Walked
the plank', 'Pushing up the daisies', 'Six-foot under', 'Bitten the dust',
'Croaked', 'Given up the ghost', 'Shuffled off', 'Gone to the happy
hunting grounds', 'Gone belly up', 'Snuffed it', 'Turf-eater' – all these
phrases allow us to talk about death with ironic humour.

   How we talk about the death to relatives and friends of those who
have died needs much more care. Just as it is unwise to crack inappropriate jokes or comments about death and dying before checking
how the person is coping, it is equally important to be prepared to
name what has happened without using euphemisms. 'Passed away',
'Gone away', 'Crossed over' or 'Slipped away' often mask an awkwardness or embarrassment for those who use these terms, because
the words 'death' and 'dying' may sound too brutal. Others use
euphemisms because they are quite simply unsure about how to talk
about death and dying.

   Nevertheless, many of those interviewed for this book found these
euphemisms irritating. As one interviewee commented bluntly, '*Died*
is a perfectly valid word for the state of no longer being physical
among us. People should use it.'

   'Euphemisms sound silly,' said a second, although she did agree
that people used them 'to soften the brutal impact of the reality of
our fragile little lives'.

Others were more vocal in their dislike. 'They should all be banned,' said another interviewee. 'My usual response is to say something back that involves saying "died".'

Some were particularly irritated by the phrases 'Passing over' or 'Passed away'. 'If you were dying, you wouldn't say "I'm passing away", would you?' exclaimed one interviewee. 'Passed over bloody where?' said a second. She went on, 'When people talked about me losing my father, I wanted to respond, "No, I have not lost my father. I know exactly where he's buried, thank you." I wanted people to say my father had died – otherwise his death loses its meaning.'

Another interviewee said that 'passing over' made her think of spiritualists in the 1920s, table-tapping. She also mentioned the euphemism, 'Gone before'. 'What', she asked, 'does that mean? Gone before what?'

Others said they found euphemisms with religious connotations frustrating, such as 'Gone to heaven', or 'God loved X and wanted him/her to come home', or 'He/she's in a better place now', especially when the person speaking had no belief or faith.

A psychotherapist expressed concern about well-meaning but mis-guided people saying to a recently bereaved parent, 'At least you have got two other kids – you need to think about them now.' Or 'Never mind, you are young enough to have another one.' 'This thoughtlessness', said the psychotherapist, 'usually suggests the person can't really handle talking about death, and would rather just make everything better. Of course they can't and this kind of com-ment only makes things worse.'

People also expressed concern that the euphemism 'Gone to sleep' could be very misleading for a child. A funeral director joked, 'Ter-rible to take a sleeping person to the crematorium and pile earth on them. There ought to be a law against it!'

Another funeral director believes that using euphemisms only compounds the fear of making a mistake or using the wrong word. But he admits that the funeral industry is full of such language. He actually heard one funeral director say to a bereaved family, 'We will conduct a hygienic preservation to facilitate the visitation of the loved one in our chapel of repose.'

This is a hard act to follow, so I will conclude with my own abhor-rence of 'Loved one' – for some reason, a creepy, hand-wringing Uriah Heap always springs to mind, and anyway, maybe the 'loved one' was downright horrible. And this comment from someone whose mother died recently: 'Personally', she said, 'I like *dead*. It just sums up what happened to her.'

What to take from this

- Respond to those who are bereaved in their own language. Listen and be sensitive to how the person may want to talk about death and dying.

- Check how someone is feeling *before* making assumptions.

- Encourage children to be honest and open about their own thoughts on death and dying.

Not everyone experiences grief

We also need to be mindful that not everyone who has been bereaved is willing or ready to express grief, as a BBC journalist experienced when reporting on a disaster.

I will never forget covering a ferry disaster. I got to where it happened as quickly as I could and walked into a café, searching for people to interview. I noticed a man sitting at a table with a group of others, talking quite normally. He was having a cup of coffee in the sunshine, looking clean and tidy, as if nothing out of the ordinary had happened.

As I listened to him it dawned on me that he was one of the survivors and his wife had been killed. They had been sitting together at a table on the ferry, when it seemed as if the place had suddenly become a lift-shaft. He held onto the table and his wife did not. He survived because the table was screwed to the floor.

He told me the story as if he might have asked you to buy him a cup of coffee. No emotion, and I don't believe he was in denial either. It was so different from the expectation of bereavement we impose on people. He was very contained, coping extremely well at the time – and in his own way – without doing what we, the media, want people to do. That taught me a lot.

Of course, the man from this disaster would have been in shock, and it's possible and even likely he fell apart later on. What matters, however, is how the journalist respected and met the person where he was at the time.

It is equally important to appreciate that for some, the death of a close relative is not distressing or even upsetting.

Roz, an eco-adventurer who rows across oceans to raise awareness of climate change, did not feel grief-stricken after her father died, but sometimes felt guilty when other people expected her to.

> I don't remember any awkwardness when my father died. Maybe it's because I wasn't upset, and people picked up on the fact that it was okay to talk about it. It just wasn't that big a deal in my life.
>
> Strangely, the only times that I have felt awkward have been when someone has assumed that I missed my father as much as they missed theirs, and asked questions such as, 'How was I coping?', 'How do I go on?', 'How do I deal with the grief?' But there wasn't any grief. I wondered if it would come up and surprise me one day. Four years on that still hasn't happened. I don't think I'm burying it – I just don't think it's there. But at times it's made me feel embarrassed that I was not more grief-stricken.

Roz now believes that most grieving is not about the person who has died – they are past pain and suffering – but it's about the gap that person has left in the lives of the still-living. 'However,' she said, 'I do understand that grief is a natural reaction for those left behind, and when expressed properly, it can be very cathartic.'

Personally, I empathize with Roz. I grieved the death of my mother well before she died. I remember one day looking at this little bent old lady and thinking, I have lost my Mum. I went to bed that night and cried for hours. When she finally died, I felt very little sadness. I was just glad her suffering had come to an end. For me, her death felt like a release.

I felt little grief either when my father died. As I noted in the introduction to this book, our relationship was difficult, and I often struggled to find positive ways to communicate with him. And yes, it was hard to witness this bull of a man end his life in such a vulnerable state. But the time we had together in hospital enabled me to say my farewells, and to wish him well as he died in front of me. His funeral, for me, was a very jolly affair, especially seeing lots of faces from the past who clearly loved him. But I did find it irritating when some people came up to me and said, 'I am sorry for your loss.' My response was, 'Well, I'm not sorry. He had a good life and he didn't suffer. I am relieved he died the way he did.' I know they were well-meaning, but it would have been much better if they had *asked* me how I was, rather than *assuming* how I was. However, I would also say that it is better to speak to someone who has been bereaved than not at all.

Any difficult feelings I had after my father died were concerned, mostly, with no longer having parents. This realization would hit me in waves at the oddest moments. At first these waves were seismic, but they tailed off into a gentle swell that rolls over me every now and again.

What can help

- First of all, check-in with the person. Ask them how they are with the death of their relative or friend. This allows the person to tell you how they are grieving, or whether they are okay with it.

- You may not feel comfortable with their response, but it's important to let the person have *their* experience.

- Knowing how they are can help to open up a more honest conversation.

Breaking bad news

To conclude this section, it's important to look at how to break bad news. When done badly it can have a disastrous effect. For example, someone had such an awful experience when he was told about his terminal illness by a doctor, that he refused to engage with further treatment. Another was informed by his consultant that he was 'riddled with cancer'. The patient was devastated – not just by the news, but by the heartless manner in which the news was delivered.

A third example was given by Hazel, the mother of four boys, who experienced the dreaded 'knock on the door' at seven o'clock in the morning. A young policeman had come to deliver the news that Adam, her 19-year-old son, had been accidentally killed during the night.

> My 21-year-old son opened the door to him. The policeman asked him to wake me up. I came downstairs thinking, 'Oh dear, one of my boys has obviously got into a spot of trouble.' The policeman didn't ask us to sit down, he just launched in by saying, 'Adam is no longer with us.' It took a moment to understand what he was saying, before my son and I screamed in shock. The policeman quickly added, 'Well, we're not sure. It might not be him.'
>   This totally confused us. I asked the policeman what he meant. He replied, 'We can't confirm it is him until he's been identified. But we've been to the address he had in his wallet, and he wasn't there.' He then said, 'We would have come sooner, but we had to conduct investigations to make sure he hadn't been pushed or he hadn't committed suicide.' The policeman then gave me some telephone numbers, told me who to contact, and left. His visit had taken less than 20 minutes.
>   I was completely shocked, not just by this awful news, but the way in which the policeman delivered it. He had had no training. He clearly didn't want to do it, and he couldn't wait to leave. I was horrified that we had been abandoned like this.

Ten years on, Hazel no longer feels angry about what happened. She was fortunate enough to have very supportive family and friends, which helped her get through the following minutes, hours, days and months. 'But', she said, 'what would have happened if I had been on my own, or I had fallen over from the shock? My advice to anyone who has to break this kind of news is first to ask the person to sit down, and as quickly as possible tell them what's happened in plain language. And don't leave until family or friends arrive to take care of them.'

Thankfully, since Hazel's experience, the police have radically changed their approach to breaking bad news. Throughout the police force in the UK, Family Liaison Officers (FLOs) are now specially trained to deal with this, and are setting an excellent example for other institutions and individuals to follow.

Breaking bad news guidelines

Whether you are unfamiliar to the person, or a close relative, friend or carer, should you find yourself in the position where you have to break bad news, the following guidelines may help. They have been adapted with grateful acknowledgement from the approach used by the Metropolitan Police in London.

- It's important to remember that the manner in which bad news is delivered will stay with the person for the rest of their life. Therefore, it is best to break bad news face-to-face. Even when this is not possible – the closest relatives may, for example, be abroad – be sensitive to the impact that this news will have on the person at the other end of the telephone.

- For more information for deaths that happen abroad, go to the Metropolitan Police Force website (www.metpolice.co.uk). Under 'A–Z' list go to B and follow links to Bereavement advice.

- This is probably one of the most important things you will ever do. For face-to-face conversations, it helps to prepare yourself by rehearsing what you are going to say, especially if there may be language or disability issues. The health of elderly people also needs to be taken into account.

- Don't delay giving the message, *especially* if the death could attract media attention.

- Give yourself plenty of time when you are with the person, and make sure you break the news, as far as possible, in a safe and confidential setting.

- If the person doesn't know you, make sure you identify yourself first. *Use plain language* so the person won't get confused about the reason you are there. Your opening sentence could be, for example, 'Hello, I am Sue. Are you so-and-so (first name and surname)? I am sorry to say I have some bad news for you. Let's go inside and sit down so I can tell you what has happened.'

- Encourage the person to sit down *before* you break the news. This helps to contain them. Sometimes people can become so distressed that they could lash out. Remember, your welfare as deliverer of the message is as important as the receiver's.

- If possible, make sure there are no interruptions. Switch off mobile phones and telephones, and turn off radios and televisions.

- Stick with the task in hand. *Use plain, simple language*, and don't waffle or bring in unrelated issues. This can cause confusion. You may say, for example, 'I am so sorry to tell you that (name) has just died.'

- In the case of a sudden death, you may say, for example, 'I have some very difficult and distressing news to tell you. (Name) has been killed in a car crash. It happened this morning.' Then tell them everything you know *at that time*. This will change as time passes and more information is known.

- In the majority of cases, people who hear bad news will only be able to take in a small amount of what is being said. So validate what they understand has happened, and encourage them to have their feelings. Gently correct them if necessary. Be prepared to repeat yourself and *write down* important information, for example, where the body is, or how to contact the coroner, or who to contact at the hospital.

- Don't swamp the person. They may need physical space to take in this news. Leave it up to them if they want to be touched or held.

- *Don't promise anything that you can't deliver, or commit to anything you can't carry through*. This will destroy trust.

- If possible, don't leave the person on their own. Ask the person who you can contact on their behalf. Or you can ask for their phone book to find someone who lives nearby. Whenever possible, stay with the person until family or friends can take over.

- *It can be very distressing to deliver this kind of message*. Make sure you take care of yourself once you leave the person. Police FLOs have a buddy system for each other. But if you are on your own, do think of a good friend whom you can confide in.

CHAPTER 8

A Practical Guide to Support the Dying

> Patients are, usually, much more ready than most of us realize to talk about dying. What they need is opportunity and permission. That is why it's now time for a change in the social culture of death, with more discussion and information so that everyone is better informed and can choose to prepare – in good time – for an event that will be easier to navigate once ignorance, myth and taboo have been deleted from the equation.
>
> Hilary Lovelace, Palliative care nurse

Until now this book has looked at the experiences and views of health professionals, faith leaders, relatives, friends and carers on how they find ways to talk about death and dying.

This chapter sees a change of emphasis, with hands-on guidance and advice for anyone who is currently facing the dying process of a relative or friend: from saying goodbye and the importance of good listening skills, to recognizing end-of-life experiences and what happens at the moment of death.

This chapter is an amended amalgamation of two booklets (*End-of-Life Experiences: A Guide for Carers of the Dying*[1] and *Nearing the End of Life: A Guide for Relatives and Friends of the Dying*[2] produced by myself and Dr Peter Fenwick to help relatives, friends and carers to provide better support for the dying.

Palliative care professionals know that dying can be messy, wretched, uncomfortable and devoid of any outward signs of spiritual, or even positive, experience. However, they also know that many deaths are peaceful, calm and serenely joyful, involving 'non-ordinary' experiences that can hold profound spiritual meaning to the dying and/or those who bear witness to them.

The dying experience may involve any combination of the above states, and move between them. But, as we have already explored, the way people deal with their dying process is often a reflection of how they have conducted their life and handled other challenges and major life changes.

No matter how experienced you are with the dying process, you are constantly learning. No two deaths are the same – and you have to be prepared to be caught off-guard, even when you think you know what is happening, and everything has been discussed openly.

Sometimes touch, music, candles and flowers are appropriate. Sometimes just a place of calm and acceptance is needed. At other times there is a need to cry and get angry.

Although it can be beautiful at the end, dying in its early stages can be dreadful – even horrific. And it is naïve to expect, need or hope for someone nearing the end of life to have some kind of revelation of love, or a spiritual experience.

Some have completed their goodbyes and have found peace. Some want to be left alone. Others may well have moments of glory or revelation as an essential part of helping them to let go. Being a companion to the dying is about being sensitive to *their* needs, not your own. This means being willing to be open, and knowing when to intervene or ask questions and when to stay silent and wait.

Judith Pigeon
Co-founder of the Transitus Network

Of course, the dying need appropriate physical pain control. But, as mentioned earlier, they also have what might be termed soul needs – to feel heard, cared for, connected and emotionally safe. They want to be understood and accepted like anyone else.

Some people are fortunate in being able to approach their dying process at peace with themselves and with those they love. But that's not always the case. People can be frightened, confused, and unable to express what they're feeling or what they need.

- They may be afraid to die.
- They may feel they are a burden to you, to their family or to society.
- They may be raging at the thought of being cheated of life.
- They may feel lost and alone, and desperate for someone to ask how they truly feel.
- They may feel angry and let down by God.
- They may be clinging on to hope for a miracle cure.
- They feel as if they have wasted their life and be grieving missed opportunities.
- They may be desperate to die.
- They may want to make contact with ex-partners or estranged family or friends.
- They may want to confess to things that have happened in the past, or to ask for forgiveness. This can be painful and upsetting for relatives, but it can also be powerfully healing.
- They may also become irrationally angry, blaming and resentful towards you, the medical and nursing staff, or the world at large.
- They may be missing relatives and friends who are unable to be with them.
- There may be nothing much going on at all. People usually die as they have lived. So, for some, this can mean a quiet and uneventful death.

If your relative or friend is becoming anxious or upset and you feel unable to deal with this, do talk to the nursing or home-care staff. The person may not be able to tell you exactly what's going on for them. Indeed, they may find it difficult to understand themselves.

It's also important to understand that a dying person often chooses who they want to talk to. This may not be to a nurse, doctor or relative. It could be, for instance, the cleaner who calmly gets on with their daily task, or it could be a junior member of staff, or a volunteer or pastoral carer with whom the dying person has built up a rapport.

SAYING GOODBYE

When the end is near, most people tend to want a bottom-line, no-nonsense handling of the situation. However, I have seen families in complete denial of the impending death, who refuse to participate in anything that sounds like concluding affairs. 'No Dad, you are going to pull through this. We don't want to hear about wills or insurance papers.' And the family turns its back on the dying person's very real need to settle accounts.

Megory Anderson
Author of *Sacred Dying*

Do your best to be there for the person who is dying, in any way that you can, but make sure you take care of yourself too. You may feel okay about being alone with the dying person. You may want and need company. But be aware that some close family members may find the thought of sitting with their dying relative too upsetting.

Saying goodbye in person is an important process for everyone. With gentle encouragement and support, anxious or frightened relatives can often overcome their alarm and find comfort in having sat at the bedside.

Some who are dying know what is happening to them. Nevertheless, when a dying person believes relatives and friends can't cope with the truth, it can be hard for them to talk about what they're experiencing, or ask for what they want or need. This can leave the person feeling isolated and lonely, not knowing how to reach out or say goodbye.

So, how can a meaningful conversation happen? Those who are dying sometimes help indirectly by throwing out 'tester questions' to check if you are willing to engage with them. They might, for example, ask you, 'What do you think happens to you after you die?' They might ask if you think there is life after death. They may ask, 'Do you think God really exists?'

On the other hand, you yourself may want to broach the subject of death with your relative or friend, but don't quite know how, especially if death has never been mentioned before.

One of the easiest ways of opening up the subject is to ask your relative or friend who they would like you to contact if they became very seriously ill. This conveys that you know they may not recover and are willing to talk about it. It also gives them the space to decide whether or not to respond.

If you don't feel quite ready to have this kind of conversation and you're in a hospital, hospice or care-home setting, talk with the nursing staff so they can offer appropriate support. If you are at home, talk to the GP, district nurse, community nurse or the Macmillan nurse.

> Heiner's friends clearly didn't want him to be sad and were trying to take his mind off things. They watched football with him just like they used to do; they bought beers, cigarettes, had a bit of a party in the room. Some of them even said, 'Get well soon' as they were leaving: 'Hope you're soon back on track, mate!'
>
> But no one asked me how I was feeling. They don't get it. I'm going to die.
>
> Taken from *Noch Mal Leben Vor Dem Tod*, 2004

HOW TO LISTEN WELL

The most important gift you can give to a dying person is to listen. Here are a few golden rules of good listening which can help you open up communication:

Be respectful   None of us truly knows what is going to happen after death, whatever our religious or spiritual beliefs. So it's important not to force our viewpoint onto the dying person. This is *their* dying experience. It's our job to bear witness and not to judge.

Be honest   Often in difficult situations we tend to search for the 'right' or clever thing to say. Or we deny what's happening, or make a joke of it. While such reactions are very understandable – humour has an important place too, even in death – dying is a profound process that just needs us to be there, and perhaps hold a hand. The act of sharing ourselves openly and honestly can be both liberating and soothing for the dying person.

Engaged body language   Don't be afraid to look your relative or friend in the eye. Be alert and attentive to what they are telling you and the way they are saying it. Listen to their tone of voice and be aware of changes to their facial colour, their willingness to engage with you, their willingness to meet your eyes.

Is what they are saying really what they mean?   Are they asking you something with their body language that they are not expressing with words? If so, invite them to tell you what they really want to say. For example, 'I noticed you looked upset when you said that. I wonder what's really going on for you?'

Try to put your own thoughts aside   It's easy for your attention to be emotionally hijacked by thoughts about this person, your fear about them dying, or perhaps by something else that is happening in your life which is preoccupying you or causing you distress.

You may also feel embarrassed by this kind of emotional intimacy, or fearful of seeing your relative or friend cry, or become helpless and vulnerable. Breathe slowly to calm yourself.

Ground yourself by feeling your feet firmly on the floor. This will help you to be present and accepting of what is happening.

Use open questions such as How?, When?, Where?, Who?, What? and Why? (although be a little careful with Why?, as it can sometimes sound accusatory or intrusive). Open questions give the message that you are paying attention and will encourage your relative or friend to talk frankly.

Use direct questions   Asking 'Are you frightened of dying?' or 'What are your fears about dying?' provides an opportunity for honest communication. However, it can take courage to put such questions to someone for whom you care deeply.

Use indirect questions   A softer approach can be to use indirect questions such as, 'I wonder whether there's anything you want to talk to me about?', 'Perhaps there's something bothering you which you want to tell me about?' or 'What can I do to help you at the moment?' This gives your relative or friend the choice to respond, or to say no. Providing choice is empowering. They may decline initially, but will know the door is open if they want to talk about it later. Indirect, exploring questions give the signal that you are safe to talk to, and that you care.

Use leading questions   You can also gently ask leading questions to find out how they are feeling, such as, 'If you become really ill, would you like me to sit with you?', 'If you become ill, what medical care would you like?', 'Have you ever thought about what you want to do with your belongings?' or 'Have you thought about what kind of service you would like at your funeral?' Again, this provides the dying person with the choice to respond or not.

Use short statements   These can also provide comfort. You might say, for example, 'If there ever comes a time when you want to talk about something or you feel frightened, please do tell me.' This gives your relative or friend permission to talk in his or her own time, without expectation.

It's okay to cry   Crying is a natural response to emotionally charged situations. Being brave enough to express your grief can have a powerful healing effect on your relationship, as well as giving your relative or friend permission to grieve for the life he or she is leaving behind.

Don't feel you have to talk all the time   Just sitting quietly at the bedside is important, and can often be surprisingly peaceful.

LIFE REVIEWS

Many people who are approaching death find that Life Reviews help them validate what has happened during their lifetime. Going though old letters and photograph albums with them can be particularly healing. Some set themselves clear objectives to complete and they may need help to accomplish this. Others may begin to question their religious or spiritual beliefs. Or they may find solace in old or new faith.

A lot of people, especially older people, are happy to talk about their wills and what they want to happen after their death. So it's about finding ways to open up these conversations. One way is to ask the person how they would like to be remembered. Another is to help them go through family jewellery or precious possessions such as pictures or china, and see who they want to leave it to.

Or you could begin to reminisce about someone who has already died. By saying, for example, 'It was really sad when Granddad died, but isn't it lovely to be able to talk about him now. He had a lovely funeral. Is that the kind of thing you would like too?'

However, it is important to know that patients often experience periods when they believe they are going to live for ever. This doesn't necessarily change when they reach the end of life either.

So it's about being sensitive to know what's okay in any given moment. Good end-of-life care is really about listening to what each person wants and needs – and respecting that for some, denial is their coping mechanism.

Professor Sheila Payne
Help the Hospices Chair in Hospice Studies, Lancaster University

THE DYING PROCESS

There are certain signs that indicate when illness or old age has tipped into a preparation for death.

Physical changes   These changes are part of the ageing process. The skin can appear paper-thin and pale, with dark liver spots appearing on hands, feet and face. Hair can also thin and the person often physically shrinks in height. Teeth can discolour or develop dark stains.

Their external world begins to diminish until the dying person no longer wants to leave the house or their bed.

Increased sleep   The person begins to sleep for long periods. This can be distressing for relatives, but it's important to understand that physical exertion for someone approaching death is exhausting and, for the moment, all effort is being put into staying alive. Nearer the end, they may increasingly drift in and out of consciousness.

Appetite reduces   The body knows it no longer needs fuel to keep it going, and those who are dying often lose their desire to eat or drink. They can begin to lose weight, sometimes quite rapidly. It's important not to force food or drink onto someone who no longer wants it. But do take guidance from the nursing staff.

Change of language   The person may start to talk about 'leaving', 'flying', 'going home', 'being taken home', 'being collected', 'going on holiday', 'packing a suitcase', or making some kind of journey. They may also begin to express heartfelt gratitude to their carers and their family as a preparation to saying their farewells.

Special requests   They may want something special, such as to visit a particular site, or be surrounded by their favourite flower, or to hear certain music, or to have family photographs near, or to make contact with someone who has been important in their lives.

Josefine's story

My father urged my dying mother to eat, but she didn't want to. She told him, 'I don't have to work anymore.' He accepted this, because trying to feed a dying person is like watering a dying plant.

She mostly slept. But every so often she became agitated, distressed and very anxious, which made it difficult for her to breathe despite having oxygen. It felt as if her anxiety attacks were like going into labour – and they were painful birth contractions. We sat her up.

My Dad looked into her eyes and told her: 'You are my angel, you always will be my angel!' She weakly smiled at him, and then she calmed and lay back on her pillow. Eventually she could no longer speak, but she conveyed to us she wanted to look out of the window at the trees and parkland which surrounded the hospital.

We moved her bed to the window and she found the will and energy to sit on the edge of her bed for several minutes, looking out at the parkland. Then she settled back into her bed peacefully. The next evening she died, with my father's sister and me sitting by her bed, him gently bending over her, telling us how they had first met.

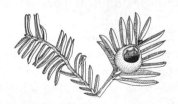

END-OF-LIFE EXPERIENCES

The more veiled becomes the outside world, steadily losing in colour, tone and passions, the more urgently the inner-world calls to us.

Carl Jung

The dying experience is often emotionally exhausting for relatives and friends, especially if they have never been with someone dying before.

However, research tells us that even though the dying may be confused, semi-conscious or unconscious, many have powerful end-of-life experiences, which not only help them to let go and die at peace, but also help ease the grieving process of relatives and friends who witness them. These fall into two categories:

Transpersonal end-of-life experiences

These possess other or transcendental qualities which cannot easily be tied into the pathology of the dying process. They can occur weeks and days before the person dies and also at the moment of death. They include:

- Deathbed visions. For example, seeing much-loved deceased relatives, or sometimes religious figures or even pets who seem to have come to 'collect' the dying person.

- The ability to drift between two worlds. These other worlds are often described as wonderful, peaceful, extraordinary and seem to prepare the person for what is coming.

- Profound waking or sleeping dreams, which help the person to understand they are dying.

- A sense of love and peace filling the room shortly before, during or after the person has died.

- Deathbed coincidences, where relatives or friends who are not with the dying person but perceive the time of death before they are officially informed.

- Other phenomena are also reported such as clocks stopping synchronistically at the moment of death, and the appearance of animals, birds or butterflies at the moment of death, which appear to be significant to relatives and friends.

The male patient asked us to stand one on each side of him because he wanted to thank us for looking after him. He then looked over my shoulder towards the window and said, 'Hang on, I will be with you in a minute, I just want to thank these nurses for looking after me.' The patient repeated himself a couple of times, then he died.

Peter Fenwick and Elizabeth Fenwick, *The Art of Dying*

Final Meaning end-of-life experiences

Final Meaning end-of-life experiences appear to have substantive qualities, firmly based in the here and now, which call the dying person to make meaning and to resolve unfinished business.

These Final Meaning end-of-life experiences can begin several months before a person dies. For example:

- A dying person experiences the desire to take stock, becoming aware of issues in their lives which may not have been resolved.

- They might feel an urgent need to reconcile difficult family relationships, or broken friendships.

- Sometimes they need to ask for forgiveness from those they feel they may have wronged.

- A pressing need can be felt to come to terms with inner conflict or past traumas.

- They may have an urgency to put their affairs in order, such as sorting out a will, or finalizing their funeral arrangements.

Dreams

Dreams often appear to play a significant role in the dying process. These can be sleeping or waking dreams, where the person is transported as it were into a 'parallel' existence, and can often mark a change in the patient's behaviour. For instance, following one of these dreams, a patient who may have been expressing anger and agitation with medical staff and/or relatives, can find a sense of peace and comfort, which helps them to let go.

Some dreams seem to inform the person they are going to die. Other dreams appear to help the person to process unfinished issues. This example was given by a medical professional who worked in a palliative care team:

> An elderly Jewish woman had a very distressing dream in which she experienced being raped on Euston Station by German soldiers. The dream or vision was so real that she became very agitated, and even wanted to make a complaint to the hospital authorities. To calm her, she was given medication. However, it wasn't until her son spoke to the medical staff that the deeper significance of the dream emerged. During the war, Germans had raped members of her family, prior to them being gassed. The patient, however, had escaped. So for her this dream – or vision – was based on reality. The interviewee called the Rabbi who spent a considerable amount of time with the patient, helping her to come to terms with what had happened to her family. The interviewee believes this was a classic ELE because the dream had helped the patient to become reconciled with what had happened to her family and relatives before she died.

Dreams also happen to relatives and friends.

It is not unusual for family members and friends to dream of the person who has died. One interviewee described a dream where she saw her dead father as a young man. He was smiling at her and waving goodbye to her.

Another interviewee, whose wife had been tragically killed in an accident, said that shortly after she died, she came to him in a dream to tell him she was okay and would be waiting for him. This was greatly comforting for the husband.

A third interviewee had a very powerful dream which enabled him to find a sense of completion with his father who had recently died.

> My father's death was what might be called a good one, but prosaic and physical rather than spiritual or existential. In his late eighties, he had lung cancer and, with a little help from morphine, he went relatively quickly and without much pain.
>
> I'd never had a particularly close relationship with him. But, six weeks after his funeral, I was bowled over by the most wonderful dream experience, in which the father I'd never really had came to

me, suddenly and dramatically, aged about 55 (close to where I am
now), and surprised me in the middle of an entirely unrelated dream.
Startled, I turned towards him, and saw the kind, smiling, strong, confident father I'd always longed for. 'Dad!' I said, feeling an overwhelming physical as well as emotional joy, 'you've come back!' 'Yes,'
he replied, 'I needed to, to say goodbye.'

'I'm sorry I wasn't at your funeral,' I replied, 'but that was for reasons I know you understand. And now we can truly say goodbye.' We
embraced, and it was as if his body was merging into mine as I
absorbed the essence of him, his masculinity, his wisdom, his age, and
took on his mantle.

It was one of the most extraordinary dreams I have ever had and
shook me awake. I lay for a while, assimilating what had happened
and wondering briefly if this had been some kind of supernatural
visitation. No, I realized. For me, this was a closing of a psychological
circle, a finishing of unfinished business, and without doubt a
transpersonal end-of-life experience. My father hadn't had that in his
own death. I did it for him – or rather, the experience was offered to
me as an act at some level of grace.

There are countless stories about the power and mystery of dreams,
although it is not known how many dying people have such dreams
or end-of-life experiences. But research does suggest that they
happen in all cultures and religions. It is probable that many end-of-
life experiences and visionary or mystical dreams are not reported,
because:

- The dying person is afraid of appearing confused or distressed,
  or believes he or she will be given medication to stop these experiences.

- Carers may keep quiet about them because they feel it is not
  professional to talk about such things. Or they simply do not
  have the time to sit with the dying, and therefore miss them.

- Relatives may not speak about such experiences to staff or to
  family and friends for fear of ridicule or disbelief.

There is no such thing as a 'normal' death. Everyone dies in their own unique way. Nevertheless, research suggests that when people do have these end-of-life experiences, they can be enriching, not just for the dying person but also for those relatives, friends and carers who witness them.

Whether dying persons are telling us of a glimpse of the next world or conversing with people we can't see, we can consider ourselves blessed when it happens. If we don't make the mistake of assuming they are 'confused', we are likely to feel some of the excitement they convey.

For we are witnessing the momentary merging of two worlds that at all other times remain tightly compartmentalized and mutually inaccessible. That merging is what I mean by the spirituality of death.

L. Stamford Betty
Are They Hallucinations Or Are They Real?

How to tell the difference between end-of-life experience or drug-induced hallucination

The difference between genuine end-of-life experiences and drug-induced hallucinations is usually clear to nursing staff and to patients.

People who have drug-induced hallucinations might describe such things as the wallpaper moving, the carpet undulating, insects crawling up walls, strange animals walking around on the floor, or devils or dragons dancing in the light.

They may 'pluck' at their sheets or at the air, and shiver. These hallucinations are generally experienced as annoying rather than frightening, and doctors can control them with medication.

In contrast, people who have end-of -life-experiences seem to be calmed and soothed by them. They appear to help the person let go of the physical world and overcome their fear of dying.

What should I do if my relative is having – or not having –
an end-of-life experience?

Renate's story

My husband refused to admit he was dying. He fought it right until
the end. I was with him when he died. It had been an exhausting
time for us both.

But, as he took his last few breaths, I saw his face light up with
delight and amazement. It was very moving. I am sure someone he
knew and loved had come to collect him. It certainly helped him to
let go.

These end-of-life experiences are real to those who have them, so
listen without judgement or dismissal. It is important to remember
that this is something they are actually experiencing, and that it is not
for us to say whether it is authentic or imagined.

It is crucial that the dying person's reality is supported. Practise
your listening skills (page 120) to help your relative or friend know
you really care about what is happening to them, and that you are
willing to hear about it. Tell them how much it means to you to know
they are being reassured, even if you are unable to share their visions.

Put any disbelief or prejudices aside and truly listen. Help them by
asking questions such as, 'What does he/she look like?', 'How many
have come to see you?', 'What does it feel like, or look like?'.

If your relative or friend is not having this kind of end-of-life experience, that doesn't mean they are having a 'bad death'. We don't
and can't completely know what goes on in the mind of a dying
person, or what they may be experiencing while asleep, confused or
in a coma. Reaching out a caring hand can be very reassuring, as
well as quietly saying words of farewell.

It is also important to know that some people become distressed
by seeing end-of-life visions and by having dreams which tell them
they are dying. Take their distress seriously. Tell the nursing staff and
they can, if necessary, provide medication to help relax and soothe
the person.

What happens if my relative or friend has dementia?

Judith's story

When my mother was suffering from the terrors of Alzheimer's, rarely being 'in this world', she recovered sufficiently to have a day of complete clarity with me, when we were able to say all we needed to say.

On the final day, just before she died, she murmured something which meant she was making a reconciliation with my dear husband (with whom she had a difficult relationship), which in turn allowed me to move forward.

Dementia or severe cognitive impairment is a growing issue in the elderly. More than 100,000 people die with dementia in England and Wales each year. Research suggests the overall prevalence of dementia in those over the age of 65 is about five per cent. This increases as people enter their seventies and eighties.

The impact dementia has on the dying process can be confusing and alarming. It can be difficult and sometimes impossible to reach the person, or understand what they are saying or what they may want.

However, there are many reports of those with severe dementia suddenly becoming lucid enough to say farewell to those around them, or talk coherently about seeing dead relatives.

So don't dismiss everything they say as disjointed ramblings. And be available in case this person does return to clarity and wants to make a final connection.

Mark's story

I was present with my fiancée at the bedside of my future mother-in-law. Hers was not an easy death. She seemed to find it hard to let go because she was crying out and sounding very confused. But for me, the experience was strangely gentle, and also rather prosaic.

Eventually, we noticed that her breathing had altered. We called the nurse into the room and she confirmed that she was dying. We held her hands and I could feel the warmth and life ebbing out of her body from her limbs upwards, until the final breaths about 15 minutes later.

She had always been very private about her fears around dying. But hers was, despite the distress of her final days, as good a death for her as we could reasonably have hoped for. This was the first time I had been at the bedside of someone as they died, and I'm very glad I was there.

What should I do if I can't be there at the end?
When it's not possible to spend time with the dying person, you can still feel connected to them. Memories of someone who is dying or has died are often bittersweet. These reminiscences become part of who you are, and can influence how you choose to live your life. Therefore it's important to find something that helps you achieve a sense of completion.

You might, for instance, want to create a special space where you can light a candle and say prayers – or whatever you need to do – to say goodbye.

Perhaps write them a letter expressing the things you wanted to say but never did. If they have already died, you might want to burn the letter ceremonially or bury it.

Maybe you need to go into nature to say your farewells, or to buy a special tree or flower and plant it in their memory.

My work as a funeral director is about helping families to transform a fact – that someone has died – into a ritual that is authentic and relevant to those who were close to that person, to help them say goodbye in public and with meaning. Planning a funeral is a chance to help someone turn their grief into something beautiful, where – as a family – they can come together and create an event that reflects how they feel about the life of that person.

They can do something grand, something eccentric, something useful, or just sit quietly with their feelings. This makes new memories for everyone, and provides a chance for others to come and share the grief, in whatever way it happens. Some people can do this with their grief. Others need to collapse for a while and have someone else do it for them.

Even so, there is still an expectation in our society, particularly for widows, to behave 'frightfully well' at the funeral. This means at one point said widow taking out a tissue and delicately dabbing one side of her nose.

Other cultures behave completely differently. For example, Muslim women hold their heads while they scream and sob at the graveside. That's not on the British menu. But, rather than just following the British widows' blueprint, there are certain rituals you can create which can help to express feelings in a way that is comfortable. Talking honestly about the person who has died rather than sanctifying them certainly helps. Or perhaps making or writing something special to put on the coffin, or in it before it is cremated or buried.

It's also about getting the balance right for the whole family and providing each person with an opportunity to say their farewells in whatever way is okay for them – as well as for the person who has died.

James Showers
Director of the Family Tree Funeral Company

Funerals are, of course, central to the grieving process. They allow us to share our grief and to take part in an established social and personal ritual of saying goodbye, surrounded by others who also knew and loved the person.

However, it's also important not to feel guilty if you have little or no love for the person who has died. You may have experienced a difficult or abusive relationship with them. Or you may have felt abandoned or betrayed by them. So, rather than grief, you may feel relief that they have gone. This is also entirely okay as a reaction.

Nevertheless, if you find you are struggling with your grief, or holding onto unresolved feelings for this person, do consider talking to a bereavement counsellor.

BEING THERE AT THE END

Accompanying someone to the point of death is a remarkable experience. Nonetheless, you may find the anticipation of waiting for them to die emotionally and mentally exhausting. At times you may fervently wish for it to be over. You can feel guilty for thinking like this. But it is a normal and understandable response to a stressful situation.

Here are some points and suggestions which may help.

- Hearing is thought to be the last sense to go, so never assume the person is unable to hear you.
- Talk as if they can hear you, even if they appear to be unconscious or restless.
- If possible, lower lighting until it is soft, or light candles, making sure they burn in a safe place.
- Try to keep bright sunlight away from their face and eyes.
- You can create a peaceful, soothing atmosphere by playing a favourite piece of music or songs softly in the background.
- You might wish to quietly read a favourite poem, or a spiritual passage or religious text that means something to them.
- Strong physical contact can be painful or invasive. It is best to sit beside the bed and gently hold their hand.
- If appropriate, arrange for end-of-life prayers to be said by a chaplain, vicar or priest, or by other faith ministers (for more inter-faith information, see Chapter 4).

The use of gentle touch

Gentle touch can provide comfort for the dying and help communication on a deeper level. Even when a person is unconscious or semiconscious, they might be able to respond with faint pressure from their thumb, for example, or twitch a toe.

A light massage using aromatherapy oils such as rose, geranium or lavender can soothe and reduce discomfort and distress. Those who are dying can also find gentle hand and foot massage relaxing and calming.

Claire's story

My friend was awe-inspiring in how she put all her affairs in order and planned her own funeral arrangements. We sang songs and laughed until the end came. The biggest lesson for me was that, although she appeared deeply unconscious – she hadn't spoken or stirred for a number of hours – she could still hear.

A nurse came in to check on her and loudly said to me 'She is on her way now. She can't hear you and is in no pain.' At which my friend opened her mouth and loudly said, 'I can and I am!' Her final words. She never opened her eyes or spoke again. So I think it very important to be aware that a dying person may well keep their hearing, even when it may appear they have lost all senses.

When she was declared dead, the nurse lit candles and scattered petals on her pillow and made her look beautiful. One of her requests to me had been to always make sure that she smelled sweet throughout the dying process, so I had given her French perfume and, over the last few days, had dabbed this on her wasted body.

She had a desire to eat chocolate, so chocolate was bought and she ate as much as she wanted.

I believe she found tremendous support and strength in having someone with her who had the same spiritual outlook as herself. She knew that I could, and did, cope.

Choosing the moment to go

> You get times when people suddenly seem to perk up just before they die. They seem to get better – enough sometimes to say good-bye to a relative. It's really strange. It's like an extra energy that they've got just prior to them dying. They become coherent – and then they seem to just go.
>
> It's almost like they know – and they are waiting for someone to come. Sometimes they will just hang on until the person gets there. The person can just walk into the room and they go. It's like they wait for the time to be right for them. It's strange, but it happens a lot.
>
> Care-home carer

More than we realize, people appear to choose the moment to die. They seem to know who is strong enough to face the moment with them, and to protect those who aren't.

It is not unusual for someone to hang on to life against medical odds until a relative or friend arrives at their bedside, or until a special anniversary or birthday. As mentioned before, a person who is confused, semi-conscious or unconscious may become lucid enough to be able to say a final goodbye before dying.

Some relatives may feel compelled to visit the dying person in the middle of the night, or experience being 'called' back to the beside, for example, from a coffee break, just in time to be with them as they die.

In contrast, some people seem to make a deliberate choice to die alone. We have collected many stories of the dying who appear to wait until everyone has left the room – even for the shortest time – before they die. This can leave the relative or friend feeling either angry or guilty. However, it's very important to understand that it's not about you. The person may need the emotional space in which to feel okay to die. So take regular breaks just in case the person does want to die alone.

There are many accounts of the dying seeming to choose to die with only particular people in the room. It can be difficult when someone dies just as you have taken a break from being with them for many hours or even days. You may feel hurt that they haven't 'chosen' to be with you at the moment of death. Or you may feel guilty for believing you have let the person down by missing the crucial moment.

Heather's story

I was looking after my partner who was dying of cancer at home. His best friend would often come and sit with him, giving me a break. The evening my partner died I felt he was desperate for me to leave him with his friend – which I did. He died a few hours later. But I realized that he wanted to die with his friend who he had known for over 25 years, whereas we had only been together for three.

It may help to know that sometimes a person needs emotional freedom to die in peace on their own or, perhaps because emotions are running high, they choose to die in the presence of other relatives or friends who are more able to cope with it.

Jane's story

When I was with my father while he was dying, I had been there most of the night. In the early morning, having checked with the nurses, I went to have some breakfast. As soon as I got there, they phoned to say he had died.

The same thing happened with my uncle. I was with my aunt while he was dying. We went to get some lunch, and he died. I felt there was something here about some people being able to die at a time when they weren't being 'held back' by the people they loved. Mind you, I did feel cheated when, after all that being with him, I missed the actual departure, and I know my aunt some 12 years later still had a lot of regret about not actually being present when her husband died.

Regarding this, it was very important to me to do some ritual about actually saying goodbye. He (my father) did not want any funeral or suchlike, but I really needed to do something to acknowledge his life and his going. So I took his ashes out to sea and scattered them from the boat – he had been a naval man. There was then a sense of completion about his going.

My aunt was 74 when my uncle died and had never seen a dead body before. So I took her to see him; this was very important for her, having missed the actual death. I think the ritual of the funeral was extremely important for her. She kept some of his ashes and still has them with her.

WHAT HAPPENS PHYSICALLY WHEN SOMEONE DIES?

It is impossible to predict exactly when death will happen. People can hover between life and death for a long time, and it is easy to miss the final moment. There are certain signs which indicate the person is preparing for death.

Congestion in the lungs   The person's breath becomes laboured and 'gurgling', which can sound alarming. However, this is quite normal and caused by secretions pooling in the back of the throat.

Yawning   Even when unconscious or semi-conscious, the person may often yawn. This is a natural response to draw more oxygen into the body.

Coldness in the limbs   Sometimes the person's hands, arms, feet and legs become cold, with the skin colour changing to a pallid yellow as blood circulation slows down. However, this may not happen until right at the end.

Tea-coloured urine   The lack of fluid intake and the kidneys beginning to shut down, means the person's urine will become concentrated and tea-coloured. It may also have a pungent smell, or cease altogether.

Incontinence   As the muscles of the body cease to function, there may be a loss of bladder and bowel control. With patients who are unconscious, nursing staff will insert a catheter.

Agitation and restlessness   Dying people who are confused or semi-conscious can become quite distressed. They may also cry out. Nursing staff will often give medication such as morphine to calm them down.

Dark bruising   As the body system slows down, blood may coagulate, or pool, particularly at the base of the spine, with patches which look like dark purple bruising.

Smell   The shutting down of the dying person's system, and the changes of the metabolism from the breath and skin and body fluids, create a distinctive acetone odour. Be aware that this will happen, and that it may at first be uncomfortable for you.

No longer responding   The person can no longer speak even when awake, and will take rasping breaths through an open mouth. This can sound like loud snoring and can be very disconcerting to listen to. It also makes their mouth dry. You can help to ease this by gently wiping mouth and lips with a damp cloth.

Breathing pattern change   The person can alternate between loud rasping breaths to quiet breathing. Towards the end, the dying will often breathe only periodically, with an intake of breath followed by no breath for several seconds, and then a further intake. This is known as Cheyne-Stokes breathing. This can be upsetting to witness, as the person seems to have ceased breathing only to start again.

WHEN DEATH HAPPENS

David's story

As I watched the death of my partner, his 'consciousness' appeared to lift out of his body steadily over a period of days – with the process appearing to accelerate in the last few hours of his life.

It started with his feet, moving upwards. His head and upper body were the last areas to appear animated by his 'life force' before his consciousness finally separated from his physical shell.

I sat with my partner's body for some hours after the moment of physical death. I felt as if my vigil was supporting the departure of his spirit, and it also gave me an opportunity to let go and begin my grieving process.

In medical terms, the dying process is viewed as a biological closing down of the body's systems. It is difficult to know during this process when the person's consciousness dies. However, when death happens, it happens very quickly. There is no doubt about what is taking place. Sometimes the person will give several outward pants as their heart and lungs stop. Others may give a long out-breath followed quite a few seconds later by what seems another intake of breath. This may be repeated for several minutes, which can be alarming if you are not ready for it. However, this is only the lungs expelling air.

Other indicators are very clear:

- There will be no pulse.
- Skin colour rapidly drains to a sallow yellow.
- Facial expression changes, or loosens. You may feel you don't 'recognize' the person anymore. Some people look remarkably at peace.
- There is a sense of no one being 'home'.
- The moment of death can be experienced in many ways. It can be an intensely spiritual encounter.
- Alternatively, it may feel rather prosaic. The essence of the person has gone, leaving behind a body that can seem like an empty envelope.

Denise's story

I knew that my father was going to die that day and decided to leave him alone with my mother. I had no problem leaving him as he had told me he was 'ready to go', wasn't frightened and was very calm. We spent a lot to time talking while I nursed him and, without actually saying it, we had said our goodbyes.

I wandered around until I just felt that he had died, returning home to find he had indeed died 20 minutes before. I felt mixed emotions of relief, as he was no longer suffering and fearful. I had not seen a dead body before. I stood nervously, with my back to the wall, at a distance, plucking up the courage to approach.

It was then I felt the pressure of hands on my shoulders and a voice whispering in my ear, 'I'm OK.' This was followed by the overwhelming sensation of a very strong force moving far away with immense speed.

I knew it was my father. Any fear I had I felt melt away. It gave me the strength to deal with the duties associated with death. Much later, I realized that this experience had removed my fear of dying.

You may feel grief. You may feel numb. You may feel relief. It may feel like an anti-climax – especially in a hospital or institution, where nursing staff may be coming in and out to deal with necessary practicalities.

If it's what you want, staff may also leave you alone for a while with the body – and that can be both reassuring and sometimes unexpectedly peaceful. Sometimes, those present report less immediate physical experiences.

Carers and relatives may talk of seeing vapours leaving or hovering over the body. Others, as mentioned before on page 125, have described loving light filling the room, or a sudden change in room temperature. Or there may be heaviness in the air which takes time to clear. Or there may be other strange phenomena such as the appearance of animals, birds or butterflies.

Relatives and friends who were not there may experience 'seeing' or sensing the dead person and knowing the exact time of death before they are officially informed. These 'visitations' are usually comforting and reassuring, and never forgotten.

Or death, especially of older people, may be very ordinary and prosaic, leaving those present wondering 'Was that it?'

WHAT YOU CAN EXPECT TO FEEL IMMEDIATELY AFTER

Many relatives and friends can be very shaken up after the death of someone close. The death of a parent – even from old age – can be especially seismic, often in unexpected ways. Many also find that they tend to feel disconnected from people, places or things when they were present at the moment of death. For instance, it can feel as if you are in a dream, or looking at life through frosted glass. This can be especially difficult when you are thrown into the intensity of making funeral arrangements.

It can be hard to explain how you are feeling, especially to those who have never witnessed a death. But feeling strange or disconnected from reality is understandable when we have watched someone die. Life will never be the same again. It can't be when we have witnessed something as profound as this.

You may feel you don't know what to do with yourself. You can find yourself aimlessly wandering around, feeling lost and alone and deeply questioning everything in your life.

Over the following weeks and months, for some there may be emotional and spiritual rawness that throws up feelings of anger as well as grief. For others, it can be truly liberating. We only really know what we need to deal with as we go through our grieving process.

Avril's story

When my mother died I experienced something 'leave' with her last breath. It was, for me, quite a spiritual encounter. For several days after I also felt something intangible but very real leave me. Yet at the same time I experienced a sense of my mother's essence settling into me. It felt uncomfortable and disconcerting, and it was a couple of weeks before I felt 'me' again. In the longer term, I realized I had absorbed something of my mother's spirit, and that continues to live within me.

It was different with my father who died seven years later. At the moment of his death it felt to me more like a switching off than something actually leaving his body. I then realized that the moment of death happens in different ways.

The feelings I subsequently experienced were the same when my mother died, only sharply intensified. It was hard to accept that I no longer had parents. Even though I have a family of my own, I felt alone and as if I was no longer attached to anything – made more poignant when clearing the home they had shared for over 35 years. Much of this ended up in plastic bin-bags with a charity shop. I think that was the saddest part – and the awareness that this will happen to me too one day.

THINGS RELATIVES MIGHT NEED TO THINK ABOUT . . .

Stopping life-prolonging treatment

Many people make it known that they would not wish to be resuscitated or to receive life-prolonging treatment if their quality of life was to suffer due to a debilitating illness. For other patients, when it is clear to the medical team that treatment is not helping their condition, and that they are beginning to die, the doctors will decide to begin to withdraw these treatments (see interviews in Chapter 3).

In the case of an emergency admission to hospital, for example after a major stroke or heart attack, you may feel it necessary to inform medical staff about the wishes of your relative. However, it is important to understand that any decision to stop life-extending treatment is made by medical staff, and *no pressure should ever be put on you for this to happen*. The doctors will usually try to understand your thoughts, but they are not asking for your permission to withdraw life-prolonging treatment.

It can be very upsetting to be involved in such discussions on behalf of a relative who is unable to make his or her wishes known for themselves. So take your time to talk through any concerns you may have with medical staff, and also with other relatives.

Once a decision to withdraw life-prolonging treatment has been reached, your relative may be placed on an 'End-of-Life Care Pathway', and this will be clearly stated in their medical notes.

When initiating an End-of-Life Care Pathway, doctors and nurses focus on making the person as comfortable as possible. Fluids may be stopped and the person will receive only essential medication for the relief of distressing symptoms (pain relief, anti-sickness drugs, etc.) and nursing care such as regular mouth-care, washing and turning. Nursing staff may also insert a catheter into the bladder and give medication to ease the secretions in the back of the throat when the person is no longer able to cough.

It is difficult to gauge how long someone may take to die. For those sitting with the dying it can often feel like a very long time. You may also at times feel distressed – and even guilty – about your relative being on an End-of-Life Care Pathway. However, it may help you to know that this offers the most comfort for your relative, and support for you and your family.

Family dynamics
The death of a close relative is a critical time for families. Although it usually falls to the immediate next-of-kin to provide support and care, the dying process can bring about a togetherness within the extended family unit that usually only happens on anniversaries and

holidays. This togetherness can be – although sad – a wonderful shared experience for all concerned.

Having said that, family feuds and other unresolved issues that have lain dormant for years, if not decades, can and do resurface. This can be a very tricky time. So be aware that emotions will be running high and tempers can fray. Nevertheless, it's also important to find a way to respect and allow everyone to deal with their feelings in their own way and in their own time.

Sally's story

I had never seen a dead person. Mum was to be my first and I was uncertain how it would happen, what it would be like and how I would know when she was dead. All four of us sat together round Mum's bed, taking turns to hold her hand and chatting quietly, all individually trying to prepare ourselves for losing this important person in our lives. Around four in the afternoon, Mum's breathing became very laboured, stopped once or twice and then, finally, an hour or so later, she stopped breathing altogether and died. It was an incredibly emotional moment.

My younger sister and I wept loudly, my older sister left the room in tears to be alone, and my brother stood silently at the end of Mum's bed, just staring at her body in disbelief. I shall never forget it. It was an honour and privilege to be there and share that experience with my family.

Family members can react differently. For example:

- Some will have had a warm relationship with the dying person. Others may be harbouring dislike, grudges or anger.
- Some will freely embrace what is happening. Others may want to deny that the person is dying.
- Some will be happy to stop life-extending treatment. Others may not want this.
- Some may feel horrified or even sickened by the person's deterioration and find it difficult to sit with them.

- Relatives who live at a distance may feel guilty for not being there. Others may avoid contact due to family conflict.
- Relatives who care for the dying person may feel that their own life is on hold and become angry and resentful with the rest of the family for not pulling their weight.
- Sibling rivalry may surface and divide loyalties, causing further resentments and disputes.
- Some may be holding onto secrets that no one else knows and be finding this distressing.

So, be prepared for this to be an intense time which needs patience and understanding, and be willing to communicate openly and truthfully with the rest of the family. And be equally aware that family dynamics can make this impossible.

PRACTICALITIES TO CONSIDER

Here are a few suggestions to help you cope, whether your dying relative or friend is in a hospice, care home or hospital.

- First of all, be prepared to cancel your life. When someone is dying you will probably find it impossible to do or think of anything else apart from being with them or preparing for their death. And when you are not with them, you will be on red alert every time the telephone goes.
- You may feel as if you are walking around in a bubble, unable to relate in your usual way to 'normal' life. Everyday conversations may seem trivial and irrelevant. You may find loud, busy or noisy places like supermarkets or restaurants hard to handle.
- Explain clearly to your children and other family members what you are going through. Additional stresses and strains can feel hard to bear. Tempers can easily fray.

- Get someone to stock up the fridge and larder with ready-made meals and soups. You probably won't feel like cooking when you come home. But do make sure you have something hot and nourishing to eat every day. You need your health and strength.

- Tell friends what is happening. People are amazing when they know they can be of support and help. It is comforting to have family friends sitting with the dying person. So do offer friends the opportunity to come and say their farewells. Some will gladly do this. Others may not, preferring to remember the dying person as he or she was.

- Make sure you have plenty of credit on your mobile telephone and remember to charge it regularly. You will find yourself making and taking lots of calls from family and friends. In a hospital, this usually has to be done in an echoing corridor with trolleys and people clattering and rattling by.

- If required, make sure you have plenty of change for the car park. Some machines only take coins.

- Be very careful when you are driving, as you will be preoccupied with what's going on.

At the bedside

- It can be alarming to see the person you love attached to a syringe-driver, monitors and a respirator. It can be hard too to be with someone who is semi-conscious, in physical or emotional distress, and who may be moaning or crying out. You may yourself feel very anxious and helpless. You may also feel overwhelmed, vulnerable and lonely, especially when nursing staff are busy with other patients.

- Make sure you take plenty of breaks. It can be hard to find a private place when things get tough, but there are often quiet rooms in hospices. And hospital chapels are usually open round the clock.

- You may feel guilty when you go home knowing you might never see the person again. That's normal. Just make sure when you leave that you say your goodbyes. These farewells can mount up as the days go by.

- Most hospitals, care homes and hospices will not provide food for relatives. Sandwiches, especially from hospital vending-machines, can be pretty dismal, and to keep your strength up you will need more than just snack food, so do consider bringing in your own food. Hospital cafés can be closed at weekends and local cafés may be closed on Sundays.

- Staff are usually happy to give you coffee and tea as you sit by the bedside. But it might be an idea to bring in a thermos so you can have a drink at any time. Drinking plenty of fluids is very important, particularly as hospitals and hospices can be hot, dry environments.

- If you are in an open hospital ward, don't hesitate to pull the curtain round to get some privacy. Let the nursing staff know that's what you want to do.

- Bring in a comfortable pillow and blanket – especially if you are staying overnight. Hospital chairs have upright backs and are extremely uncomfortable after a couple of hours. If your relative is in a hospital side-room, you may be able to bring in a bed-roll so you can sleep on the floor. *But check with the nursing staff first.*

- Don't be afraid to knock on the hospital Chaplain's door. They can also arrange for a priest, rabbi or ministers from other religions and denominations to come and talk to you, or to say end-of-life prayers with you and your dying relative or friend. They will often come in the evening, if appropriate, to say prayers with the dying person even when you may not be there.

- Let the nursing staff get on with their job of providing nursing care. It is usually best to leave the room when they are washing and making the dying person comfortable. But don't be afraid to ask staff to provide extra mouth-care or turning, or to inform them when your relative becomes distressed.

- Don't be afraid to ask nursing staff if there is anything you can do while sitting with the dying person that might help to keep them comfortable, e.g. mouth-care. But remember that just being there is often a comfort in itself.

- Above all, don't be hard on yourself. This is a very difficult and challenging time. Phone calls and visits quickly become part of your daily life, and the process can seem grindingly endless. But remember that in comparison to the dying person's life-span, their dying process is a short, precious time for you, and for them.

SUGGESTIONS FOR FRIENDS

Khemanandi's story

It can be very difficult for friends to know how much they are needed or what they can do. I discovered this when my friend, who was from the same Buddhist community as myself, was dying in hospital of a particularly virulent sarcoma. Even though I was one of the people in her life who she trusted, I couldn't work out how important I was to her. But I was also aware that her children were struggling to cope with the sudden onset of her illness, and her siblings who lived at some distance were also coping with the death of their father.

I also found it really hard to know what to do for her, especially when she became irritated that I couldn't make her oxygen work better and we waited hours for her bed to be changed. I decided to leave but, looking back, I wish I had stayed. But I do not regret leaving her with her brother and sister on the day before she died. I think all three found this a great comfort.

I arrived a few minutes after she had died. Her siblings were clearly ready to go, so I went into the room to sit beside her body and to meditate. I felt a lot of grief being confronted by the undeniable reality of her un-living body while I was doing this.

It's difficult to put into words exactly what happened next, but as I was sitting there I felt a tremendous surge of liberation and freedom. It was a state of consciousness that certainly wasn't just mine.

I also felt a flood of relief that her suffering was now over. And around all this a huge amount of love.

It then began to subside. Shortly afterwards, another Buddhist friend turned up. He sat down on the other side of the bed and read a passage from the Tibetan Book of the Dead, after which we had a cup of tea, sharing the tenderness of the moment, then we left.

I have never forgotten that feeling of liberation and freedom, nor have I ever encountered such intensity before or since. But I do believe that by staying in the moment with my friend's body I was able to tap into a sense of flow and change that took me to the edge of something incredibly powerful. It certainly challenged how I identified with my perception of everyday consciousness.

It is important for you to be able to say your goodbyes to your dying friend. Even so, for some families it can be difficult to accept friends being present during the dying process. Other families will be delighted and relieved to have you there. You may need to feel your way through this. Providing the right kind of support to relatives of the dying is important, as well as being non-judgemental about how relatives and other friends may be emotionally affected by what is happening. It's little acts of kindness that count and will be remembered.

What to do

- As a friend, check with the family if it's okay to say your goodbyes in person. You may want to do this on your own, or while family members are present. Just let them know what you would prefer.

- If you are able to, offer to sit with your dying friend. This can be very comforting for families. Be sure you feel able to provide this support, as being with someone who is dying can be hard, emotional work.

- Send regular short texts or emails to relatives, without expectation of an answer. It is comforting for the family to know you are thinking of them.

- Offer to baby-sit, cook meals for the family, or to fetch and carry youngsters to and from school. You may be needed to take other relatives to see the dying person.

- Don't take offence if you are not wanted. The offer of unconditional help is often enough.

What not to do

- Don't send 'Get Well' cards when you know someone is dying. It can be very upsetting for relatives or even for the dying person to read them.

- Don't expect relatives to spend hours on the phone talking to you. They will have enough to do caring for their dying relative.

- Don't expect relatives to engage in conversations that do not revolve around the dying person or the care they are getting.

- Don't ask questions of a dying person who is too ill to respond. It can be stressful for them to try to communicate with you.

- Don't be falsely jolly. Be sensitive and be yourself.

LOOKING BACK

Many of those interviewed for this book felt pretty battered and bruised after their relative or friend had died. Because of this, they were keen to talk about what helped them to cope – and what did not – in the hope that their experiences could provide support to others going through similar situations.

What helped
Families willing to be honest
Several years ago Rose cared for her partner who died at home from terminal cancer. She was helped by her partner's willingness to discuss what was happening.

My partner's acceptance of the fact that he was dying and his clarity
of thinking made it easy for us to talk through how he felt. Exploring
the whole experience together in depth – while in some ways awful –
was an amazing experience. So honesty, openness and time together
were important keys.

Rose added that her partner's willingness to talk meant that medical
staff could be 'open, frank, calm and quietly supportive' about the
way they supported Rose and close family.

Margaret, who now runs a bed and breakfast, was in her mid-forties
when her husband died. She was also relieved when her husband
spoke openly about his terminal diagnosis. It helped them to take
the decision to give up their hotel business so they could spend time
together.

It helped that both of us were prepared to face the truth that he was
going to die. We decided to spend lots of time together. We wanted
and needed to reminisce about our life – the happy and the sad
times, our mistakes, our friends and enemies, death and dying.
     We went back to South Africa where we had met, and were joined
by our two sons. We cherished every second even though all of us
suffered serious bouts of overwhelming anger and grief. But it gave
us the opportunity to look back on the old times, as well as discussing
a future without him.

Margaret is grateful for the truthfulness the whole family shared. It
gave her many treasured memories, and the strength to care for her
husband as he died.

Judith was brought up in a family in which death and dying were
spoken about openly. Part of her grandmother's work was to lay out
those who died in the community, so for Judith, death was an
accepted part of life. This helped her to cope with the emotional distress of her mother dying.

What helped the most was having an acceptance that nothing more
can be done, and a recognition that death brings up a mixture of
feelings such as guilt, love, fear, loss. I also found the staff very helpful and supportive, especially when they recognized my exhaustion.

Robert and his family found that it helped their relationship with hospital staff when he said he knew his father was dying.

It helped that Dad had been a doctor – he had taken a decision not to have further intervention. There came a point when we were told by a young doctor he was really unwell. I was able to help her along by saying, 'What you are telling us is that he is dying?'. She and the rest of the medical staff were profoundly relieved that I had said the word 'dying'.

Spiritual or religious belief
Karen has profound spiritual beliefs, which helped her to make decisions on the best way to support herself while her mother was dying.

The best decision I made was asking a healer to be with me as my mother died, so she could say the words I couldn't. I wanted to tell my mother to go to the Light, and to surrender to it. But I found that as the time neared it became much harder. So I asked a healer to be with me while my mother died and say the words for me. It really helped to accept she was dying and being there with her.

Positive attitude from staff
When Jennifer's grandfather died in hospital, she was greatly comforted by the care he received from nursing staff.

The staff spent time talking to him, and showed great sensitivity even when he was in a deep coma. It felt as if they still saw him as a person, even though he was dying. The doctors also gave me an anticipated timescale for his death. I found this very helpful. I am a person who likes to know what to expect.

Brigitte often visited her brother who died of leukaemia while both were in their teens. She has never forgotten the kindness and compassion of the nursing staff.

What helped were those nurses who were bright and sunny and cheerful and said things like, 'So you have come to get your brother treated.' They also explained cancer to my brother, which was a relief to my parents because they didn't know what to say to him.

Anita, who runs a charity, also experienced kindness and under-standing from nursing staff on the many times she visited a much-loved close relative.

> It really helped being allowed access to my relative whenever I wanted, and in whatever state I was in at any given time. People just being with me when I was distressed, without trying to talk me out of it. One person said he couldn't know how I felt, but hoped I would be gentle with myself. I found that very kind.

Clare travelled to Barbados to be with her friend, who died of ter-minal cancer in a hospice. She stayed with her friend until the end and was deeply touched by the care and support she received from a nurse.

> The nurse who was looking after my friend was fantastic. Her attitude towards my friend's impending death was completely matter-of-fact and accepting that life was a continuing cycle of life and death – like a wheel. When my friend started to die, she said, 'She's on her way now.' After my friend had died, she spread petals all over her pillow.

Clare concluded that 'Being with the dying needs to be a time of hon-esty and truth, because if we aren't able to say what we really want to, it will be too late.'

Other things that helped

Alison's father died in a private hospital wing. She was particularly grateful for the privacy that her father and the whole family were able to have while he was dying. It meant they could spend as much time with him as they wanted to. (If your dying relative is in an open hospital ward, talk to the nursing staff about moving them to a side room as soon as possible. This does, however, depend on what's available.)

Jane found that her training as a midwife helped her to deal with her father who died of chronic cirrhosis of the liver.

> My father was an alcoholic. However, because of my nursing training, I knew what to expect, and was prepared when my father collapsed

in a nursing home. What helped me was knowing about terminal care, and reading a lot on the subject.

After Linda's father died, she found ways to talk about him with her children, which comforted her.

Following his funeral I found sharing memories of my father, by looking through photographs and listening to tape-recordings with my children, very comforting.

What didn't help

Lack of empathy from staff
Although many of the interviewees spoke warmly about the kindness and compassion of nurses, some were angered by a lack of empathy and understanding from medical staff.

Alison, whose father died in a private hospital, is still angry about the care he received from his physiotherapists.

They ignored him when he asked to be put back into bed. They said he would have to sit in the chair for at least an hour. But, when the time came, they didn't have the staff to move him. He was in agony, crying in pain and begging to be able to lie down again. But they continued to ignore him and treated him like an errant child. Whether he was dying or not, he deserved to be heard and his pain acknowledged. It marred his last days, and we never received an apology for the way he was treated.

When Jane's father collapsed in the care home, she had a difficult time trying to communicate with a hospital doctor about her wish to stop life-prolonging treatment so her father could die with dignity. Her experience illustrates the complexities that often surround such a difficult decision, especially when the end-of-life requests of the dying person are not known, and relatives and medical staff are unknown to each other.

My father was rushed to a nearby hospital. On my arrival I requested the Consultant not to proceed with any procedures which might prolong his life. My father was 77, an alcoholic with very little liver function left, on top of which he was suffering from pneumonia and had virtually no quality of life.

The Consultant said I had no right to request this on my father's behalf. I asked him if he knew of my father's health history. He did not – so I told him. This changed his attitude slightly. However, he said he had to give my father antibiotics intravenously as otherwise he and his team would have been guilty of negligence.

I just felt the last thing I needed in that situation was to be fighting medics in order to gain a peaceful and dignified death for my father.

Linda also experienced poor communication with hospital staff.

If felt as we had handed over my father to a machine, with us on the outside of it. His care had been factual and business-like, with no place for feelings. I was never sure when I was allowed to visit, or how long I could stay. No one talked to us, so we never got to know any of the staff. The doctors were vague too, so we never knew what was going to happen.

Going back to the ward where he had been didn't help either. My father asked me to do this – to say thank you – but there was no one there who had cared for him, and of course his bed was now occupied by someone else. I found it terribly impersonal and sad.

Although Jennifer was more than satisfied with the care given to her grandfather, she was horrified, when hospitalized for a short time, to witness the lack of care given to an elderly patient.

I was put into the same ward as an elderly lady who was clearly dying. She was left alone all day. None of the medical staff spoke to her or tried to communicate with her while they were monitoring her. I found her isolation very difficult to bear.

The contrast of care received by her grandfather and that of the elderly patient still continues to trouble Jennifer.

On the morning that Brigitte's brother died, her parents were summoned by the hospital authority to be told that a doctor had made a serious error.

Before he died, a junior doctor made a fatal mistake on the amount
of chemotherapy my brother was given. It caused my brother a lot of
unnecessary suffering. The Head of Department called my parents in
on the same morning my brother died to tell them what had happened. He also handed over my brother's medical notes so they could
see the evidence.

Brigitte's parents were shocked at the way this had been handled.
Instead of getting upset with the doctor, Brigitte said her parents felt
they were being used by the Head of Department. They strongly sus-
pected he had called them in to protect himself. So they made the
decision not to take future action. They hoped the doctor would
learn from his mistakes and go on to provide really good palliative
care.

Negative responses
When Clare's friend was dying, she found the hardest thing to cope
with was other people's emotions.

Sometimes people would visit more out of duty than choice – their
fear would be noticeable and you could see they couldn't wait to
leave. My friend was very aware of this, and hurt by it.

Rose, who cared for her partner until he died at home, agreed with
this.

What did not help was people who couldn't talk and/or arrived with
very long faces. We needed some joy, humour and lightness of heart
to help us get through the day. Spending time trying to 'cheer up'
others was not my priority but did, in the end, take up a lot of time.
   Family responses ranged from speechless disappearing acts, to
wanting to do something – anything – to help. Sometimes this was
great. Sometimes it was very difficult to cope with.
   After he died, I received endless calls checking to see if I was all
right, but which really involved me reassuring them. I found this
exhausting and, on occasion, counter-productive.

However, Rose was quick to point out that, although she was
often emotionally drained by friends calling, if people hadn't called

she would have found that difficult too. So it's about getting the balance right between expressing concern and needing support for your own grief.

Anita found that the most unhelpful responses were from those who told her they knew how upset she was.

> At times I wasn't particularly upset. I also didn't like people hugging me so I felt restricted, or saying things like 'You poor thing.'

Not being honest
Anna also found it unhelpful when a doctor avoided saying the word 'cancer' when assessing her relative's condition, very different from an oncologist (cancer specialist) who explained exactly what was going on and how serious it was. 'I found his directness very helpful', she said.

For Judith, it was those who avoided talking about what was really happening, or were unable to accept her mother was going to die.

> They said things like, 'How could you let her die and not make her live!' It also did not help when I was informed that if my mother didn't go into hospital she would be in agony and terrified, and I wouldn't be able to cope.

Difficult family dynamics
Karen was particularly distressed when her relationship with her sister became strained.

> My sister arrived, not having seen my mother for many weeks. She immediately started to say that my mother's lips were too dry, and why had I let it get like this. I was so angry, the matron took me aside and said, 'Don't worry, those who haven't been around for a while are often like this.'

The matron's words helped Karen realize the complexity of reactions that different family members feel, especially when a parent is dying.

SUMMARY

- It's okay to be afraid of facing the death of your relative or friend. But the gift of being prepared to be there with them is priceless. It is so much easier when everyone concerned is open and honest about what's going on, and willing to work together. It can get very tense when this doesn't happen.

- If you are concerned about the care your relative is receiving, do say something to the staff. They are there to support you, but sometimes you may need to tell them when you don't understand something, or when you are unsure of how to handle different situations.

- Life doesn't stop when someone close becomes terminally ill. You may be coping with all sorts of stressful situations and can end up feeling like a pressure cooker ready to explode. Anything can set it off, from the death of a much-loved pet, to washing-up liquid running out. So you will need to find safe strategies to let off steam.

- Give yourself time off, even if you can only manage the odd hour. This becomes especially important when the person becomes progressively ill. You may find your life taken over by doctors' appointments, hospital visits and results from yet more medical tests. Use any time you have to nurture yourself so you can build up much-needed inner resources.

- It's much easier to handle a stressful situation when you are feeling well. So make of a point of exercising and eating healthy food. Drink lots of water and, if possible, cut down on alcohol and coffee.

- Remember just how awkward many people, and even medical professionals, are with death and talking about the dying experience.

- Medical staff may talk to you about ending life-prolonging treatments. It's important to appreciate that this is not your decision to make.

- Try as far as possible to make sure that the dying person is cared for in a quiet and peaceful environment.

- Be aware that when a close relative – especially a parent – enters their dying process, it can bring up unresolved family issues that may have lain dormant for a long time. Therefore, things can sometimes become quite volatile between family members.

- Be willing to be open and receptive to your relative or friend wanting to talk about their dying experience. If you feel you cannot do this, do talk to carers who can support you.

- Listen to what your friend or relative wants or needs, and try to ensure that those needs are met.

- Listen to what the dying person is describing during the last weeks and days of life, and be supportive to whatever is happening for them. It is *their* dying experience.

- Help to create a sacred space as they enter their dying process – perhaps with gentle massage, lighting candles, or playing beautiful music.

- Remember that hearing usually continues to the end for the dying person. So don't be afraid to talk to them.

- If appropriate, be open to being there at the end, knowing that this can be one of life's most enriching experiences.

- You may – or may not – experience strange phenomena around the time of death and directly afterwards.

- After being with someone who has died, be aware that you may feel strangely disconnected from reality for a period of time, and that you may find yourself asking questions about your own life.

- If at any time, and especially after several months, you feel caught up with grief and unable to move forward, do seek help from a professional counsellor.

Notes

1   Generously sponsored by the Sheepdrove Trust.
2   Generously sponsored by the Aim Foundation.

A Few Final Words . . .

I hope this book will help you find ways to talk more openly and honestly about dying, and to face the death of someone close. It's such an important part of life, and for our own personal development and growth. But it is down to individual choice whether we deny the D-Word, or we consciously turn round and face it squarely in the eye. I have certainly elected do the latter, which is why I want to know as much as I can about the D-Word.

I want to be connected to who I am as I approach my death so that I can make every moment count. But if destiny has an abrupt end in mind for me, I want to be ready for that too. I certainly do not want to waste my last few seconds thinking, 'Damn, I wish I had said this, or done that.' Rather, I want to be able to fling open my arms and declare, 'Well, that was one hell of an experience. Here we go!'

And climate change is upon us. We don't know exactly how this is going to take effect, but globally things are pointing towards a pretty rough time for us all. We need to be ready for this, and to accept, whether we like it or not, that we *have* to deal with the D-Word. In the coming years, I think there's going to be a lot of it around.

To each and every one of you who have reached out for this book and read this far, I wish you well on your journey of life as it brings you ever closer to the ultimate experience – the D-Word.

What Can Be Done to Tackle the D-Word?

I asked interviewees for their thoughts and ideas about different ways in which we could learn to talk more openly and honestly about the D-Word. Obviously, the following cannot speak for society at large. However, I would suggest that these recommendations may represent what many others would like to see happen.

Bereavement support

- Much more open acceptance of the pain and grief.
- A much clearer understanding of the whole grieving process.
- More education and support on how to talk to a bereaved person.
- More awareness campaigns about death and dying.

Education in schools

- End-of-life education to be introduced at school and included in, for instance, Citizenship discussions, debates and websites.
- Allowing children of all ages – if they want to go – to visit mortuaries as part of their life education.
- Encouraging palliative care nurses, funeral directors and bereavement counsellors to give talks in schools.

Government policy

- Compulsory making of Wills and Advanced Directives (Living Wills).

- People to be given the choice of how they would like to die. (At the time of writing, issues concerning choice at the end of life are currently being reviewed by the Medical Regulator.)

- More working parties led by end-of-life carers who work 'at the coal-face'. They need to be listened to, rather than placated or ignored.

Health education

- More awareness about how unresolved grief can create illness.

- More education and acceptance of the inevitability of death.

Media support

- More focused articles in newspapers and magazines as well as frequent debates in the media.

- More realistic portrayal of death.

- Special training for journalists and presenters to feel comfortable when talking about dying.

Medical training

- Specialized end-of-life training for GPs, doctors and nurses.

- A ban on euphemisms and medical jargon.

- The creation of mediators who can help relatives and friends to understand what is happening during different phases of the dying process.

- Better training for GPs to recognize the symptoms of bereavement, which are often diagnosed as depression.

- More specialized death and dying counselling available through GPs.

- Compulsory end-of-life training programmes to be delivered to anyone (professional, volunteer and all support staff, including cooks and cleaners) who work with or alongside the dying.

Public education

- Re-introduce mourning rituals.

- Tackle ignorance in a society that disregards the opinions of the dying.

How can these changes be implemented?

In order to change anything in our life, we have to take action. It's down to us as individuals how we do this. For example, the first thing to do is stop pretending that death happens to other people and set an example by making a Will *and* a Living Will. Then tell everyone you've done so.

We need to educate ourselves about the D-Word. So if you work in a professional setting and are uncomfortable when talking about death and dying, ask for workshops, symposia, conferences and training programmes which focus on end-of-life issues.

You can also write about the D-Word, shout about it if necessary. For example,

- Start up blogs or websites which can help you share your views on how to talk about dying.

- Insist that GPs and medical staff talk to you in *plain* language.

- Lobby your local MP for changes in end-of-life policies you would like to see.

- Ask for the school where your child goes to include information on death, dying and bereavement.

- Sit your child down and tell them about death and dying. Be honest with them about your own fears and beliefs and encourage them to do the same with you.

- *And*: listen to what the dying and the bereaved *really* need.

Recommended Reading

Anderson, Megory, *Sacred Dying*, Marlow & Company, 2004.

Armstrong-Coster, Angela, *Living and Dying with Cancer*, Cambridge University Press, 2004.

Barratt, W. F., *Death-Bed Visions: The Psychical Experience of the Dying*, Bantam, 1926.

Berridge, Kate, *Vigor Mortis: The End of the Death Taboo*, Profile Books, 2001.

Betty, L. Stamford, *Are They Hallucinations Or Are They Real?*, Omega, 2006.

Brayne, Sue and Fenwick, Dr Peter, *End-of-Life Experiences: A Guide for Carers of the Dying*, 2008. To order copies please go to www.d-word. co.uk.

Brayne, Sue and Fenwick, Dr Peter, *Nearing the End of Life: A Guide for Relatives and Friends of the Dying*, Braynework, 2009. To order copies please go to www.d-word.co.uk.

Cowling, Charles, *The Good Funeral Guide*, Continuum, 2010.

Connor, Kelly, *To Cause a Death*, Clairview Books, 2004.

Death, Dying and Bereavement, Open University and Sage Publishing, 1993.

Downham, Jenny, *Before I Die*, Black Swan Books, 2007.

Fenwick, Dr Peter and Fenwick, Elizabeth, *The Art of Dying*, Continuum, 2008.

Gibran, Khalil, *The Prophet*, Pan Books, 1991.

Grief, Mourning and Ritual, Open University Press, 2001.

Hancock, Sheila, *The Two of Us: My Life with John Thaw*, Bloomsbury, 2005.

Harding, D. E., *The Little Book of Life and Death*, Arkana Books, 1988.

Howarth, Glennys, *Death and Dying: A Sociological Introduction*, Polity Press, 2007.

Hunniford, Gloria, *Always With You: Facing Life After Loss*, Hodder and Stoughton, 2008.

Jupp, Peter and Gittings, Clare (eds), *Death in England: An Illustrated History*, Manchester University Press, 1999.

Kellehear, Allan, *A Social History of Dying*, Cambridge University Press, 2008.

Kübler-Ross, Elisabeth, *On Death and Dying*, Routledge, 1970.

Lakotta, Beate and Schells, Walter, *Noch mal Leben Vor Dem Tod*, Deutsche Verlags-Anstalt, 2004.

Lawton, Julia, *The Dying Process*, Routledge, 2000.

Longaker, Christine, *Facing Death and Finding Hope*, Main Street Books, 1997.

The Miracle of Mindfulness, Rider Books, 1991.

Morell, Jane and Smith, Simon, *We Need to Talk About the Funeral: 101 Practical Ways to Commemorate and Celebrate Life*, Accent Press Limited, 2007.

Osis, Karlis and Haraldsson, Erlendur, *The Hour of Death*, Hastings House, 1977.

Parnia, Sam, *What Happens When We Die*, Hay Publishing, 2007.

Rinpoche, Sogyal, *The Tibetan Book of Living and Dying*, Harper San Francisco, 1990.

Siegel, Bernie S., *Love, Medicine and Miracles*, HarperCollins, 1990.

Speyer, Josefine and Wienrich, Stephanie, *The Natural Death Centre Handbook*, Random Books, 2003.

Stanworth, Rachel, *Recognising Spiritual Needs in People Who Are Dying*, Oxford University Press, 2004.

Warner, Felicity, *Gentle Dying*, Hay House, 2008.

Wertheimer, Alison, *A Special Scar: The Experiences of People Bereaved by Suicide*, Routledge, 2001.

Some Helpful Contacts

UNITED STATES

American Psychological Association
750 First Street NE, Washington, DC,
20002-4242
Tel: (800) 374-2721 or (202) 336-5500M
www.apa.org

Association for Death Education and Counselling
ADEC Headquarters, 111 Deer Lake Road, Suite 100, Deerfield, IL 60015
Tel: 847-509-0403
Fax: 847-480-9282
www.adec.org

Americans for Better Care of the Dying
1700 Diagonal Road, Suite 635,
Alexandria, VA 22314
Tel: 703-647-8505
Fax: 703-837-1233
Email: info@abcd-caring.org

Care Connections
Helpline: 800-658-8898
Multilingual Line: 877-658-8896
Email: caringinfo@nhpco.org
www.caringinfo.org/ContactUs.htm

Centre to Advance Palliative Care
Palliative Care Tools, Training & Technical Assistance, The Center to Advance Palliative Care, 1255 Fifth Avenue, Suite C-2, New York, NY 10029
www.capc.org/

Dying without Shame, Dying without Panic
A Buddhist Perspective
www.dharma-haven.org

Elisabeth Kübler-Ross Foundation
PO Box 6168, Scottsdale, AZ 85261
Email: info@ekrfoundation.org
www.ekrfoundation.org

End of Life
Information on death and dying in the United States
www.endoflife.stanford.edu

Hospice Foundation of America
Comprehensive website on end-of-life issues
www.hospicefoundation.org

National Hospice & Palliative Care Organization (NHPCO)
1700 Diagonal Road, Suite 625, Alexandria, Virginia 22314
Tel: 703/837-1500)
Fax: 703/837-1233
Email: info@nhpco.org
www.nhpco.org

PA Health Care Decision-Making
Comprehensive website on many different aspects of end-of-life care
www.pahealthcaredecisions.wetpaint.com

Sacred Dying Foundation
PO Box 210328, San Francisco, CA 94121
Tel: (415) 585-9455
Email: Foundation@sacreddying.org
www.sacreddying.org

The Centre for Living and Dying
The Atrium, 1265 El Camino Real, Suite 208, Santa Clara, CA 95050
Tel: +1 (408) 243-0222
Fax: +1 (408) 553-0110
billwilsoncenter.org

CANADA

Canadian Association for Pastoral Practice and Education (CAPPE)
National Office, 660 Francklyn Street, Halifax, Nova Scotia, B3H 3B5
Tel: 1-866-44CAPPE or 1-866-442-2773
(Good for all North America)
Halifax: 902-820-3085
Fax: 902-820-3087
www.cappe.org

Canadian Hospice Palliative Care Association
Annex B, Saint-Vincent Hospital,
60 Cambridge Street North, Ottawa,
ON K1R 7A5
Tel: 613-241-3663 or 1-800-668-2785
Fax: 613-241-3986
Email: info@chpca.net
www.chpca.net

Canadian Virtual Hospice
Room PE469, One Morley Avenue, Winnipeg, MB R3L 2P4
Email: info@virtualhospice.ca
www.virtualhospice.ca

Palliative.info
Comprehensive information about palliative care and associated links
www.palliative.info

Palliative.org
Regional palliative care program for Edmonton, Alberta
www.palliative.org

UNITED KINGDOM

The D-Word: Talking about dying
www.d-word.co.uk

Bereavement

Cruse Bereavement Head Office
Tel: 0208 9404818
www.crusebereavementcare.org.uk

Compassionate Friends
Supporting bereaved parents and their families
Helpline: 0845 123 2304
www.tcf.org.uk

Metropolitan Police
Go to 'B' in A-Z list and follow links to Bereavement information
www.metpolice.org.uk

Winston's Wish
Helpline: 08452 03 04 05
www.winstonswish.org.uk

Coping with suicide

The Samaritans
Main contact: 08457 90 90 90
www.samaritans.org.uk

SOBS
National Helpline: 0844 561 6855
9am to 9pm every day
www.uk-sobs.org.uk

Counselling organizations

British Association for Counselling and Psychotherapy (BACP)
General Enquiries: 01455 883300
www.bacp.co.uk

United Kingdom Council for Psychotherapy (UKCP)
General Enquiries: 020 7014 9955
www.psychotherapy.org.uk

Inter-faith

The Inter-faith Network UK
Promotes good inter-faith relations
www.interfaith.org.uk/

Independent funeral services

Family Tree Funeral Company, Stroud
Tel: 01453 767 769
www.familytreefunerals.co.uk

Green Fuse, Totnes
Tel: 01803 840779
www.greenfuse.co.uk/contact

The Natural Health Centre
The Hill House, Watley Lane, Twyford,
Winchester, SO21 1QX
Tel: (+44) 0871 288 2098
www.naturaldeath.org.uk

Living wills

Directgov
www.direct.gov.uk
Type 'Living Wills' in 'Search' box

Natural Death Centre
www.naturaldeath.org.uk

National organizations

Age Concern Head Office
Tel: 0800 00 99 66 – open 7 days a week
www.ageconcern.org.uk

Citizen's Advice
www.citizensadvice.org.uk

*Commission for Social Care
Inspection(CSCI)*
Organization which sets minimum standards for care homes
www.direct.gov.uk

Macmillan Cancer Support
Head office: 020 7840 7840
www.macmillan.org.uk

*National Council for Palliative Care
(NCPC)*
020 7697 1520
www.ncpc.org.uk

Terminal Illness
Comprehensive information on all
aspects of terminal illness
www.terminalillness.co.uk/hospice-care

Media resources

BBC: How To Have A Good Death
www.bbc.co.uk/health

Channel 4: It Helps to Talk
www.channel4.com/health

Personal development

Hoffman Process UK
'When you're serious about change'
www.hoffmaninstitute.co.uk/

Index